LOVE & PROTEST

*Chinese poems from the sixth century B.C.
to the seventeenth century A.D.*

Love & Protest

Chinese poems from the sixth century B.C.
to the seventeenth century A.D.

Edited and translated by
John Scott

Versification in collaboration with
Graham Martin

rapp + whiting/André Deutsch

First published 1972 by
Rapp and Whiting Limited
105 Great Russell Street, London WCI

Printed in Great Britain at
the St Ann's Press, Park Road, Altrincham

ISBN 0 85391 180 0

To David and Jean

Zi yue: ci da er yi yi

The master said: The words should strike home and that's
          enough

The Analects of Confucius

Contents

7

v.   THE SUNG DYNASTY (Northern Sung—A.D. 960–1126:
Southern Sung—A.D. 1127–1279)

Notes:

Poems:

VI. THE YUAN DYNASTY: THE MONGOLIAN OCCUPATION OF CHINA
(A.D. 1280–1367)

Notes:

Poems:

VII. THE MING DYNASTY (A.D. 1368–1644)

Concordance
and Note on Romanization

Throughout this book all Chinese proper names have been spelt in the new pin-yin-zi-mu romanization instead of the Wade-Giles system. Imperial dynasties and certain conventional place-names such as Peking, Shantung, are the exceptions to this rule.

Since many readers familiar with Chinese verse in translation may be surprised to meet Li Po, Tu Fu and Po Chü-yi in the guise of Li Bo, Du Fu and Bo Ju-Yi, I have included the following concordance of all the major poets listed in the table of contents.

WADE-GILES	PIN-YIN SYSTEM
Ssu-ma Hsiang-ju	Si-ma Xiang-ru
Tsao Chih	Cao Zhi
Tsao Tsao	Cao Cao
Ch'en Lin	Chen Lin
Li Po	Li Bo
Tu Fu	Du Fu
Chang Chi	Zhang Ji
Po Chu-i	Bo Ju-yi
Yuan Chen	Yuan Zhen
Yü Fen	Yu Fen
Chang Chie	Zhang Jie
Ch'en Yü-lan	Chen Yu-lan
Chang Pi	Zhang Bi
Lu Nan-kung	Lu Nan-gong
Su Tung-po	Su Dong-bo
Ch'in Kuan	Qin Guan
Chang Lei	Zhang Lei
Ts'ai Shen	Cai Shen
Li Ch'ing chao	Li Qing-zhao

WADE-GILES	PIN-YIN SYSTEM
Hsin Ch'i-chi	Xin Qi-ji
Liu K'o-chuang	Liu Ke-zhuang
Po Pu	Bo Pu

Introduction

An English friend once complained to me: 'The trouble with Chinese verse is that it all sounds the same.' One of the ambitions of this book is to attempt to dispel such impressions. I hope that this collection will help to complement the work of other translators by including not only a large number of poems which have not previously been rendered into English, but also verse genres which have been mainly overlooked in the standard anthologies.

Hitherto, the *fu* or prose-poem has been largely ignored except for some of Waley's early translations, those of Professor Hughes in collaboration with Professor Hawkes, the German of Von Zach, and the French of Margouliès. Then there is that rich vein of traditional Chinese verse written in the vernacular, and practically untapped by translators, long ignored and despised at least by China's orthodox establishment. Though written in the language of the ordinary people, this type of verse was often the product of erudite though heterodox writers—cultural revolutionaries in the true sense. Within this range, we have translated a few *San Qu*, Yuan and Ming Dynasty 'popular songs', and a number of *Shan Ge*, 'folk songs' mainly erotic in nature, compiled and edited by the great early seventeenth-century folklorist, dramatist and novelist Feng Meng-long. Examples of this last genre have never before appeared in any Western language. Of course, in order to keep the book balanced, I have felt obliged to include some poems which may prove to be old friends of the reader; in any case I was often so much in love with these favourites of my predecessors in the field, that I could not bring myself to omit them.

Nonetheless *cognoscenti* of Chinese verse may be surprised by certain obvious lacunae. The omission, for instance, of one

15

of the great poetic canons, *The Songs of the South* or *Chu Ci*
is explained by the existence of Professor David Hawkes's
complete translation. Similarly in the case of Tao Yuan-ming
(Tao Qian) there are the contributions of Chang and Sinclair,
William Acker and James R. Hightower. A. C. Graham's *Poems
of the Late T'ang* and J. D. Frodsham's *The Poems of Li Ho, made*
me feel it would be otiose to include the famous Li Ho, and
Li Shang-yin, who is also included in the former work, was
omitted for the same reason.[1]

Among those poems Graham Martin and I have selected we
have tried to illustrate subtle but nonetheless important
differences in style and mood. The embittered humour of Xin
Qi-ji contrasts with and complements the charming levity of
Li Bo. Both seek release in wine, but the former reflects dis-
illusionment with Confucian values, the latter a strong Taoist
and Confucian antiphony current throughout Chinese art and
literature. For although Chinese poetry was written by
members of the privileged élite, who were, overtly, Confucian
literati, the values poetry inevitably entails no less in the East
than in the West, seem to be Dionysian rather than Apollonian
(to borrow Nietzsche's terminology). Thus, the greatest of the
Chinese scholar-poets have often turned to folklore or chosen
themes underlining the conflict between the demands of the
state and the happiness of the individual. One could instance
here Bo Ju-yi and Yuan Zhen's *feng-ci* or satirical verse.

One of the earliest poems included is 'The Northern Gate',
written down perhaps for the first time in the sixth century
B.C., and already vividly reflecting this strange contradiction.

---

[1] *Ch'u Tz'u, the Songs of the South*, translated by David Hawkes,
Oxford University Press, London, 1959.
The Poems of T'ao Ch'ien, translated by Lily Pao-hu Chang and
Marjorie Sinclair, University of Hawaii Press, Honolulu, 1953.
T'ao the Hermit, Sixty Poems by T'ao Ch'ien, translated by William
Acker, Thames and Hudson, London, 1952.
The Poetry of T'ao Ch'ien, translated by James R. Hightower, Clarendon
Press, Oxford, 1970.
Poems of the Late T'ang, translated and with an introduction by A. C.
Graham, Penguin Books, Harmondsworth, 1965,
The Poems of Li Ho, translated by J. D. Frodsham, Clarendon Press,
Oxford 1970.

Its form it that of the *Feng* (a kind of folk poem), yet it chooses for its subject the predicament of the unwilling servant of the state, the individual poet's cri-de-coeur against 'the insolence of office', a theme recurrent throughout two thousand years of literary tradition.

In translating Chinese verse one is faced with the problems common to the rendition of all foreign poetry, but in addition Chinese poetry also has a complicated metrical structure based on the tonal qualities of Tang Dynasty pronunciation.

The two main types of Classical verse are the *shi* and *ci*. The *shi*, the oldest form of Chinese poetry, is usually written with a strictly regular number of monosyllabic words to the line. The *ci*, which reached its apogee during the Sung Dynasty, is a lyric with an irregular number of words to the line, and was a poem written to a specific tune. When the Chinese talk of classical poetry they usually refer to these two forms. In addition to these there are the Han prose-poem or *fu*, and the vernacular *San Qu*; also included in this book are poems belonging to the pure folk tradition, such as the *Shan Ge*. It is a thankless task to try to create verse structures corresponding to the subtleties of these Chinese originals. Translators have attempted this, but the results have seldom proved rewarding. We therefore have not, in our translations, slavishly sought to create English equivalents of these forms, though it will be apparent to any reader that the quatrain I give below belongs to a different family of verse from the poem following on false sentiment by Xin Qi-ji. The former is a *shi* the latter, a *ci*. On the other hand what has engaged our attention is to reproduce in English the mood and tone of the original. We have been at pains to show the lively colloquial nature of the narrative *San Qu*, for instance, 'The Imperial Progress' by Sui Jing-chen.

A further problem is coping with Chinese poetry's vast store of classical reference and literary allusion, which, from the poet's point of view, was not a vehicle for exhibiting mere scholarship, but rather a means of achieving compactness. Here one is reminded of Pound's theory of poetry, that its most appropriate name is the German *Dichtung*, since this term conveys the notion of compression. A good example is 'A Warning to Censors' by Zhang Jie: (As in the poems that follow, I supply a literal version. For our finished translation, see p. 90).

Zhu-bo yan xiao Di-ye xu,
Bamboo-silk smoke ceased, Imperial enterprise empty,
Guan-He kong suo Zu-long ju.
Pass, river vainly barred Grandfather Dragon's dwelling.
Kang-hui wei leng Shan-Dong luan,
Pit, ash not yet cold, Shantung trouble,
Liu, Xiang yuan-lai bu du shu.
Liu and Xiang in fact not read books.

In the first line, bamboo and silk refers to written records, since these were the materials used for the earliest books. Pass-river is a binome referring to a particular mountain pass and to the Huang He or Yellow River. Kang-hui echoes a four-syllable expression meaning 'to bury the scholars and burn the books'—that is the First Emperor of the Ch'in Dynasty, 'Grandfather Dragon's' infamous persecution of scholars and destruction of their writings. 'Shantung trouble' is a reference to Chen She's uprising which overthrew the Ch'in Dynasty. Similarly Liu and Xiang are Liu Bang and Xiang Yu, two rival contenders for the Imperial throne after the destruction of the Ch'in; though not exactly illiterates, their pretensions were certainly other than literary.

Had this poem been translated more literally, readers would have gained the impression that it concerned itself merely with one particular sequence of events in Chinese history. This was certainly not the author's intention. Secondly, had our version been so treated, we would have had to burden the reader with a plethora of footnotes in order to elucidate historical references which are from a Western point of view totally obscure. One should remember Schlegel's sound advice—'Fussnoten zu einem Gedicht sind wie anatomische Vorlesungen zu einem Braten.'[2]

[2] Though we have stood by this dictum, I have sometimes included introductory notes prior to the actual texts of the translations in order to give the reader, where necessary, some information concerning genres of verse, authors, historical background, etc. In the case of four writers, Wang Pan, Xin Yuan, Zhang Bi, and Yu Fen, so little of interest is known about them that in each case I have omitted a biographical note.

We have therefore the paradox that what is, in Chinese, a superb use of particular reference to convey a general truth, has the effect of over-narrowing the range of meaning when the original allusions are rendered into English through either expansion or footnotes. Some other means has to be found. Hence, for instance, our own choice of title for this poem and our use of 'usurpers' in the last line. Both are attempts to illuminate the universality of the author's intention.

In one poem at least we have, for obscure Chinese historical personalities, substituted fitting equivalents drawn from Western tradition. Thus in Yu Fen's poem on p. 89 we have written: 'In exchange for the Pompadour's beauty we'd sooner a plain Queen Jane.' Again, Li Bo, in the poem to his wife on p. 72, mention's an actual officer of ceremonies, or Tai Chang, famed for his tippling. This title would mean nothing to a Western reader, but the unfortunate bureaucrat's inclusion in the poem is undoubtedly meant to be facetious, which explains our equally flippant 'Old Commissioner Flask'. Likewise Du Kang becomes Bacchus in translation.

At other times, we feel fanciful names and obscure references fulfil a definite poetic purpose. This is best exemplified in the prose-poem or *fu*, where often hyperbolic conceit and obscure name-dropping perform a function comparable, shall we say, to certain Miltonic or Spenserian devices. As in Mei Sheng's 'Seven Exhortations to Rise'—

Orator Jing Chun serves the drinks,
    Lutemaster Du Lian sees to the music. . . .
Then like a whirlwind the tunes of the south strike up;
    the melodies of lubricious Zheng and lascivious Wei
    float upon the air.
Then are summoned Lady Xi Shi, concubine Zheng Shu,
    Lady Sun-Pattern, Mistress Broken Stem,
    South Baby, Lu Zhou, Fu Yu and other lovely women
    trailing dresses of every colour,
    hair hanging like swallowtails,
    eyes provocative, bosoms hinting at
    dark permissiveness.

At times I have supplied the reader with bibliographical aid to existing studies of particular poets or genres.

—the poet's aim is to intoxicate. To transpose or omit such allusions would, we felt, tend to emasculate the poem by eliminating its mysterious and magical rhetoric.

In Xin Qi-ji's famous 'Youth Does Not Know How Sorrow Tastes' an over-romantic English equivalent was needed for what, to a Chinese, would appear a hackneyed cliché, 'storeyed chambers': (see p. 115).

> *Shao-nian bu shi chou ci-wei,*
> Youth does not know sorrow's taste,
> *Ai shang ceng-lou*
> Loved to climb storeyed chambers,
> *Wei fu xin ci qiang shuo chou.*
> To pen new verses force utter sorrow.
> *Er jin shi-jin chou ci-wei,*
> But now know completely sorrow's taste,
> *Yu shuo, huan xiu,*
> About speak, just stop,
> *yu shuo, huan xiu,*
> About speak, just stop.
> *Que dao 'tian liang, hao ge qiu!'*
> Only say 'weather fresh, a fine autumn!'

Here I should stress the point that in the third and fourth lines there is an obvious echo of Tao Yuan-ming's famous stanza 'On Moving House', of which the second line of the second verse reads:

> *Deng gao fu xin shi*
> Climb high (places, hills, towers) pen new verses
> [see second line below].

The relevant section translated by Chang and Sinclair is as follows:

> Many are the beautiful days in spring and autumn
> For climbing hills and composing new poems!
> When we pass each other, we call out cheerfully.
> If we have wine, we pour it out and drink. [sic]

Tao's poem is one of his many depicting the rustic joys of country retirement. And as far as that sort of thing goes, it's a very good one too. Without wishing to cross swords with lovers of Tao's verse (among whom Xin himself should be numbered) the trouble is that many inferior imitators had an irritating habit of climbing high places where they would remain to pen their none too new sounding verses. The satirical implication in Xin's verse is certain; and to translate it into English by 'high towers' or 'storeyed chambers', etc., does not convey his original intention. The rustic contentment inspiring the voluntary recluse Tao is worlds apart from the enforced retirement of the great patriot and one-time guerrilla leader Xin Qi-ji. The former had deliberately rejected the rat-race of official life. The latter was condemned to inertia by a government of corrupt appeasers. I do not believe for one moment, that Xin is satirizing Tao's verse. His frequent references to his predecessor make the converse more likely. Rather is he at one and the same time directing his barb at inferior plagiarists and reserving a degree of irony for his own youthful enthusiasms. The poem achieves its power through first deflating the false sentiment of the inexperienced, and then contrasting it with the reticence imposed upon the experienced by true suffering. The irony of the poem is also well brought out in the French version by Kaltenmark and T'ang in *Anthologie de la poésie classique*.[3]

The use of 'autumn' (*qiu*) in the superb bathos of the last line is undoubtedly linked visually as well as phonetically with the reiteration of 'sorrow' (*chou*). The Chinese ideograph 'autumn' is made up of rice-stalk and fire—conveying the idea of bonfires in autumn. This appears evident to the eye, but it would be dangerous to assume that it is necessarily a correct etymological explanation. The ideograph for 'sorrow' is made up of the rice-stalk and fire placed above the ideograph for heart. Autumn and heart are thus combined. Without suggesting that such 'Poundian' devices are common occurrences in Chinese verse—they do exist. This overtone in the original was an additional reason for choosing 'autumnal' in the translation of line two.

A word is needed about the Chinese preoccupation with the

---

[3] Edited by P. Demiéville, Gallimard, 1962.

poem of social comment, described by Bo Ju-yi and Yuan Zhen as *feng-ci* or 'satire'. Here it is interesting to note that this form of verse became a strong influence on the German *Gebrauchslyrik* or Functional Poem in the twenties; among writers of which were Alfred Henschke (Klabund), who translated a considerable amount of Chinese verse, and his contemporary B. Brecht.

The term *feng-ci* embraces both functionalism and satire. It belongs to a tradition almost as old as Chinese verse itself, and I have selected some predecessors to the work of Bo Ju-yi and his followers, notably Chen Lin's 'Somewhere on the Great Wall', and Du Fu's 'The Sergeant at Tong Pass'. One of the main purposes of the editing of the *Book of Odes*, we are told by the Confucian School, was to place on record social criticism and political satire. This is of course a rationalization on the Confucians' part, rather than a true explanation, as can be seen by the problems the commentators obviously faced when having to supply a didactic exegesis of a pure love lyric such as 'Dead Doe in the Clearing'. But certainly from the Han Dynasty onwards, with the establishment of the embryonic Confucian bureaucratic state, the practice of editing and collecting folk poetry occupies the attention of the ruling élite, and soon compilation makes way for imitation. This hortatory tradition of literature, inherited directly from the ancients, has been continued and adapted by the modern Communist government.

Perhaps in no other culture does didacticism become such a major concern of the literati, as it does in China. Naturally this element in Chinese literature is sometimes responsible for a plethora of banal moralizing by writers whose pretensions do not rise above the flatly conventional. At its best, however, its sense of social purpose has enriched the cultural heritage of China every bit as much as the individualistic, and even sometimes hedonistic, Taoist counter-current exemplified by such great bohemians as Li Bo and Tang Yin. Indeed, most of the major poets achieve a happy blend of both these tendencies, a reaction and counter-action producing the *Zhong-yong* or Golden Mean. In the best of this 'functional' poetry the author's sincerity is unassailable: one might instance Bo Ju-yi's 'The

Salt-Merchant's Wife' and one of his successors, Liu Kezhuang's 'Pro Patria'.

The motivation behind this tendency is best explained by comparing it to the function Camus saw for himself in his reply to the Marxist-inclined Sartre, that it is not for the writer to align himself in his comfortable armchair with historical processes, but to take sides with the governed against governors. Perhaps not until Wilfred Owen and Siegfried Sassoon can we find a treatment of military hubris as powerful as that of Du Fu in 'The Sergeant at Tong Pass'. Certainly in translating we saw the honest but over-confident sergeant's trust in his superiors to be as misplaced as that of Harry and Jack in 'The General':

'He's a cheery old card', grunted Harry to Jack
As they slogged up to Arras with rifle and pack.
. . .
But he did for them both by his plan of attack.

As in Sassoon there is an attempt to capture the demotic turn of phrase, not so as to patronize but to give the flavour of stark reality. The sergeant refers to the enemy as *Hu*, a popular term of abuse for any predatory invader. This we have thought fit to render as 'Hun', since the Huns or Xiong-nu were old enemies of the Chinese.

In such poems the Chinese literati were the true spokesmen of the ordinary people. They were taking their responsibilities seriously. This is the expression of the Confucian conscience at its most admirably humanistic.

Obviously for the reasons I have stated above, the reader seeking a representative anthology of the different periods of Chinese verse will have to excuse me. I have, for instance, emphasized some of the heterodox aspects of Ming verse, and entirely ignored the relatively undynamic Ch'ing Dynasty. My selection is thematic—an attempt to show a little of the great duality inherent in the Chinese cultural tradition.

Finally I would like to thank my colleagues and friends of the Chinese Department of the University of Edinburgh, Dr. J. Chinnery and Dr. William Dolby.

I. The Chou Dynasty
Eleventh Century B.C.
to 221 B.C.

INTRODUCTORY NOTES

The *Book of Odes*

The *Book of Odes*, or *Shi Jing*, sometimes translated as the *Book of Songs*, is the oldest repository of Chinese verse. It was probably first compiled and written down some time in the early sixth century B.C., but many of the poems recorded belong to a much older oral tradition. History has attributed its editing to Confucius. Though this is unlikely, certainly the Master admired and revered the Odes, and read into these beautiful lyrical folk songs all manner of satirical and admonitory implications, thus establishing the functional literary precedent which has remained such a dominant theme in Chinese literature every since.

The Odes belong to the corpus of Confucian classics, and have been a source of inspiration to successive generations of literary men, last but by no means least the West's own Ezra Pound.

'Dead Doe in the Clearing'

Dead doe in the clearing
White reeds entangle it
Lady's bosom plump with spring
Bold knight who plays her
Tender young tree in the forest
Dead deer in the clearing
White reeds bind it
Lady like jade:
'Slowly and gently, O gently
O do not crumple my petticoat
Do not cause your hairy dog to bark'.

From: *Book of Odes*

The Northern Gate

I go out by the great city gate,
Vast are my heart's vexations.
Shabby and cramped is my room,
My troubles are known to no-one.
  It is finished
  Heaven has done for me,
  So why talk!

The Prince's affairs hem me in,
Around me matters of state build walls.
When I come home
From every side my woman besets me.
  It is finished
  Heaven has done for me,
  So why talk!

The Prince's affairs imprison me,
Matters of state, a pile of bricks heaped up on me.
When I come home
At every turn that woman checks me.
  It is finished
  Heaven has done for me,
  So why talk!

From: *Book of Odes*

II. The Han Dynasty
206 B.C. to A.D. 220

The Historical Records of Si-ma Qian

The struggle of the noble hegemon of Chu and his upstart rival Liu Bang, the drunken ex-constable, with their contrasting personalities, has been a source of epic inspiration as fruitful as our own Wars of the Roses. The death of the noble Xiang Yu meant the permanent destruction of feudalism, as we know it, in China. Liu Bang's success established the Han Dynasty, and in one sense can be said to have insured the founding of the Confucian bureaucratic state which in one form or another was to rule China from the Han to the collapse of Imperial China in 1911.

The great historian Si-ma Qian has recorded for posterity the tragic fate of the noble hegemon. The words of his poem are to this day still sung in the traditional popular Peking Opera version of this story, identically as Si-ma wrote them in the second century B.C. Though China has had no verse epic, Si-ma's account of history with its occasional interspersed poem can rival the Icelandic saga. Certainly generations of historical romanticists continued to intersperse poetry in their narrative, and this remained a permanent feature of Chinese fiction writing.

The Prose-Poem or Fu

The Han Dynasty was the truly great formative period of Chinese imperial might and culture. During the Martial Emperor's reign (Wu Di) 140–87 B.C., the boundaries of China were extended in part well beyond their present confines—not only were peripheral peoples brought under the domination of the Pax Sinica but in turn Chinese culture was alive to new ideas and influences. The confidence of expanding China is manifest in the peculiar but fascinating literary genre of the *fu*—there is an exuberant delight in Mei Sheng's enumeration of the world's delights and pleasures, reflecting the vigorous curiosity of his age, and the opulence of court life.

The *fu* probably had its origin in the ancient Southern nation of Chu which produced the great poets Qu Yuan and Sung Yu, though it is equally likely that it was born out of the prose tradition. Much of China's early prose writing already reflected the marked characteristics of the classical literary language in its later form—the love of parallelism, antithesis, and harmonious laconic expression. There are whole passages of the philosophers Zhuang Zi and Xun Zi (a southern writer) which read almost as verse. The prose-poem could well have been a new literary vehicle with its origins more in the realms of prose than poetry, developed especially as a form of euphuistic court verse, often with satirical undercurrents. At its best it is as vigorous and exciting as the dynamic bas-reliefs in the tombs of the Han Emperors—offering us something quite unlike the quiet refinements of later more sophisticated but less adventurous dynasties. Though I feel it is secondary to the delight of the language, there is of course a definite intention in all three *fu* (and in most others) to convey a moral. But even in Mei Sheng's 'Seven Exhortations' the admonitions of the courtier are subsidiary to an intoxicating description of the joys of the chase, the power and beauty of nature and the exotic treasures of the universe. A marked erotic motivation lies behind the romantic Si-ma Xiang-ru's poem—and there is a none too subtle ambiguity in the last lines implying a facetious approach to Confucian morality. The tragic Cao Zhi's moving *fu* conveys the eternal sadness of unattainable beauty in a world where passion is forever baulked by convention.

Though the *fu* claimed many a practitioner after the Han, thereafter it seems to have been written primarily as a literary exercise, and Chinese critics have rightly deemed its later imitators a paler shade of the great Han initiators. A noted exception is the great *Wen Fu* (*Prose-poem on the Art of*

Letters), an outstanding piece of literary criticism written in A.D. 301-2 by Lu Ji, of which Archibald MacLeish says, 'Far more than either Aristotle or Horace, Lu Ji speaks to our condition as contemporary men.'

As the prose-poem is a relatively unfamiliar form of Chinese literature for Western readers, I have included a short bibliography at the end of this introduction as a guide to those who might like to read more examples by other translators.

Bibliography

Birch, Cyril, and Keen, D., eds., *Anthology of Chinese Verse*, Penguin Books, Harmondsworth, 1967. See pp. 157-75. (This includes Sung Yu's beautiful 'Wind Fu' and Si-ma Xiang-ru's famous 'Shang-lin Park (both accurately and delightfully translated by Burton Watson).

Fang, Achilles, trans., 'The Wen Fu', *Harvard Journal of Asiatic Studies* (1951), pp. 527-66.

Hughes, E. R., *Two Chinese Poets: Vignettes of Han Life and Thought*, Princeton University Press, Princeton, N.J., 1960. (For the *fu* on the Capitals by Zhang Heng and Ban Gu.)

Lu Chi, *Lu Chi's Wen Fu*, translated by E. R. Hughes, in 'The Art of Letters' (Bollingen series, no. 29), Pantheon Books, New York, 1951.

Margouliès, G. *Anthologie raisonnée de la littérature Chinoise*, Payot, Paris, 1948. (Contains several prose translations of the *fu* genre.)

Sung Yu, and others, 'Kao-T'ang Fu', plus excellent notes and introduction, in Arthur Waley, *The Temple*, Allen and Unwin, London, 1923.

Von Zach, Erwin, *Die Chinesische Anthologie*, Harvard University Press, Cambridge, Mass., 1958. (This work includes German translations of a vast number of *fu*. It is a reprint of an earlier collection.)

Mei Sheng (?—141 B.C.)

A provincial court poet to the royal princes Wu and Xiao. His 'Seven Exhortations' was the first surviving prose-poem to contain a moralistic sting in the tail; its structure served as a model to so many writers after Mei Sheng that Xiao Tong (A.D. 501–531) in his *Wen Xuan* (*The Anthology*) classifies 'The Seven' as a particular verse genre.

Traditional critics have most prized the section describing the tidal bore on the Yang–tze. This superb description of an awful vista reflects the Taoist soul seen in later Chinese landscape painting—man dwarfed yet at the same time ennobled by a realization of the powers of nature. To the Taoist, water was the 'Yin', or female vital element in life—capable in the end of conquering the solidity of the male 'Yang'. Perhaps it was a little of the same humility which inspired the otherwise confident Victorian, Trollope, when he gazed at Niagara:

'At length you will be at one with the tumbling river before you. You will find yourself among the waters as though you belonged to them. The cool liquid will run through your veins and the voice of the cateract will be the expression of your heart.' (*North America*, Penguin ed., p. 70).

Si-ma Xiang-ru (179–117 B.C.)

One of the great romantic figures in Chinese literature. Although he led a rather bohemian existence for a number of years, he eventually came to the notice of the discerning Martial Emperor who made him an Attendant of the Imperial Secretariat. Whilst at the court he composed *fu* for the imperial delectation; it is not surprising that this lofty-minded verse hardly does justice to the more colourful side of his character. Only six of his prose-poems survive, of which 'The Beautiful Person' stands in a class by itself—this has led later critics to doubt its authenticity.

Before 'making good' at the court, Xiang-ru had eloped with a millionaire's daughter, called Lady Zho Wen-jun. For some time the scandalous couple kept alive running a humble tavern where Lady Wen-jun served the drinks behind the counter whilst Xiang-ru, wearing nothing but a loincloth, washed the empties at the public trough in the market-place. Eventually father relented and more than amply compensated his daughter and son-in-law with trousseau and gifts.

Since the official history of the Han Dynasty in its *Monograph on Literature* (*Han-shu Yi-wen-zhi*) accredits Xiang-ru with the authorship of this *fu*—and in view of his unorthodox behaviour with Lady Wen-jun, I see no reason to doubt its authenticity. Perhaps it is a true reflection of his 'younger and more vulnerable years'. At all events, it is the first example of erotic writing in Chinese literature to have survived the literary prescriptions of later and less enlightened generations. Indeed its language and form have served as an example to countless masters of erotic narration. To name but two examples, both the *You Xien-ku* (*Journey to the Fairy's Cave*) a Tang short story and the Ming Dynasty's *Chun Meng Suo Yen* (*Trifling Tale of a Spring Dream*) owe the rough outline of their plots to this delightful prose-poem. Amongst the purple lines describing the lady's physical charms we find the inspiration of many a later term used by the tellers of bedroom tales.

Cao Zhi (A.D. 192–232)

Sometimes he is referred to as the Prince of Chen. This tragic poet was the third and favourite son of the great warlord Cao Cao, the Martial Emperor of Wei, which was one of the Three Kingdoms emerging after the collapse of the Han. At one time his father had thought of naming him as his successor in preference to his elder brother Cao Pi. The jealous Pi on his father's death became Emperor Wen of Wei, but never forgave Cao Zhi. Drink too seems to have played its part in adding to the Prince of Chen's misfortunes. In spite of his father's love and admiration for the most gifted of his three poet sons, Cao Zhi's unbridled behaviour and his lack of a sense of occasion were his ultimate downfall. The last straw appears to have been an instance when the Prince became China's earliest recorded drunken driver—completely ignoring all protocol he drove his chariot through his father's own Forbidden City! Both his literary and tippling proclivities have won him a particularly cherished place in the hearts of all China's great bibulous poets. Li Bo once tried to shame a stingy host by quoting the generosity of Cao Zhi who pawned his possessions to buy fresh supplies of drink:

> In time gone by, when the Prince of Ch'en feasted in the
>   hall of Peace and Joy,
> At ten thousand a quart he never stinted the revellers.
> Why must our host say he is short of money?
> (*Translated by Angus Graham*)

Though it is for his outstanding composition of five words a line poetry that Cao Zhi is primarily remembered he injected into the *fu* some of the directness and simplicity in turn of phrase that he displays in his other verse. Cao Zhi criticised his Han predecessors for 'esoteric phraseology' or *qi-zi*, and suggested, in one sense quite rightly, that to comprehend much of their hyperbolic language one would have to be a scholar of profound erudition.

Traditional commentators demonstrate the romantic nature of Cao Zhi with the following little anecdote about the background to the writing of 'The Goddess of the River Luo'. During his teens he fell in love with a young woman of noble birth called Lady Zhen. But later on she was married to his brother Cao Pi. For a long while Cao Zhi pined away thinking of her, but after a few years she died at an early age. It was then that his elder brother, whether in a rare flash of fraternal affection, or just to rub salt into Cao Zhi's still smarting wounds, gave the younger brother his dead wife's pillow. At the sight of this memento of his past love, Cao Zhi is supposed to have wept bitterly and written this *fu*, originally entitled 'In Memory of Lady Zhen', and only afterwards changed to 'The Goddess of the River Luo'.

The Hegemon's Lament

King Xiang encamped at Gai-xia with a walled stockade. His troops were few and his provisions almost exhausted. The armies of Han and the other feudal lords surrounded him. In the night could be heard the sound of songs of his native Chu coming from the enemy Han armies on all sides. King Xiang was greatly perturbed, and said:

'Can Han already have captured Chu? How else is it that they have so many of my men!'

That night the King rose from his bed, and drank in his tent. He had a beautiful concubine called Yu, in whose constant attendance he delighted, and a spirited war steed, named Chui (Dapple), which had long been his favourite mount. Thereupon King Xiang sang, with noble sadness and great beauty, this poem he had composed:

My strength plucked up mountains, alas,
   my spirit capped the world
But times were not on my side, alas,
   Dapple will gallop no more
Dapple will gallop no more
   so what can be done?
My Yu, my lady, alas,
   what will become of you?

Attributed to Xiang Yu, Hegemon of Chu,
died 207 B.C., written in the Records of
the Grand Historian Si-ma Qian (145–90 B.C.).

The Seven Exhortations to Rise

The Crown Prince of Chu was ailing and a courtier of Wu inquired after his condition: 'I have heard that the Prince's jade frame is ill at ease. Has there been any improvement?' The Prince replied: 'How exhausted I feel! But I thank you kindly for your solicitude.' The courtier then said: 'The nation is at peace, the four quarters of the globe enjoy harmony, and Your Majesty has a rich future to look forward to. I am of the opinion that you have been long addicted to pleasure, day and night without end. Evil humours have attacked you, and your internal organs are congealed. You are pallid and afeared. Your breathing has been affected by a surfeit of drink. Alarmed and troubled you rest but find no sleep. You are debilitated to such an extent that you shrink from the sound of voices. Your energy seeps away. A hundred maladies will arise. Hearing and eyesight will grow dull, anger and happiness succeed each other for no reason. If you persist in this course it will be difficult to abandon these bad habits, and your life will be imperilled. Is it not this way with you, my Prince?' The Prince replied: 'I thank you for your solicitude. It is true that, relying upon my imperial power, I have from time to time indulged myself a little, but I would not say it has gone as far as you have suggested.' The courtier replied: 'You, like the sons of all noblemen, have lived secure in the Palace apartments. At home you have had a nurse, and journeying out you have been accompanied by a tutor. If you had desired to choose your own friends you could have found no opportunity of doing so. When eating and drinking you have enjoyed rich and delicate flavours, succulent meats and the finest liquor. Your wardrobe is extensive, fine clothing as warm as a summer's day; so even were your physique as tough as steel or stone it would be hard not to be melted and broken down. How much the more so when you are but a man of bone and muscle. Therefore I say: if you give vent to the desires of your ears and eyes, covet the joys of the flesh, you will interrupt the harmony of your bloodstream. If for every trip you make, you travel by chariot, I can safely say you will end up a cripple. The pleasures of the bedroom and the passion-palace are called The Go-Between of Fever. White teeth and fine moth eyebrows are known as The Axe Which Beheads Life. Rich foods and liquors are known as The Drug Which Rots The Stomach. Now, my Prince, your flesh is too tender, your countenance pale, your limbs have no energy, your marrow has gone soft, your bloodstream curdled, your hands and feet without strength. Ladies from Yue attend you in front, and concubines from Ai follow behind. With them you come and go to banquets, venting your lusts in the twisting corridors and hidden bedrooms. Such enjoyment is like drinking poison. Dalliance of this sort is playing with the claws and teeth of a wild animal. Things have gone far enough, but if you persist much longer, even if you summoned a physician as wise as Bian Qiao to attend to your internal organs or the fabled shaman Wu Xian to attend to your external person, nothing could be done. When dealing with the malady that you are suffering from, my Prince, only the world's great sages are competent, men of profound experience and extensive knowledge, who would seize the opportunity to persuade you to a change of heart. They would be constantly at your side to guide you. And then where would you find the means to protract your pleasures, pamper your lustful notions and indulge your urge for dissipation?' Then said the Prince: 'I agree with you, but I am still unwell. When I am feeling better, I will do just as you suggest.' But the courtier replied: 'It is not by means of cautery and acupuncture that your disease will be cured, but by succinct words and excellent teaching. Do you wish to hear more?' The Prince replied: 'I would like to.' Then the courtier spoke:

*

At Dragon Gate Mountain stands a turpentine tree
   a hundred feet high to the lowest branch,
In it for ever multiply the age-rings,
   its roots spread far and wide,
Behind it towers the eight-thousand-foot peak,
   a hundred feet below it rushes a torrent,

Turbulent waves, conflicting currents wash
   its roots half life half death,
In winter it is stabbed by frost, fierce wind and swirling snow
   in summer assailed by flashes of lightning, peals of thunder,
In the morning the oriole settles there,
   the *hantan* bird cries in its branches,
In the evening the bereaved female bird and the lost male
   rest there,
Upon it the solitary snow-goose sings in the dawn
   the crane mournfully circles and cries below it.
Now the year turns its back on autumn, and winter comes:
   the master lute-maker hews it down for his instrument.
Wild silk cocoons become the lute-strings,
   the orphans' jewelry adorns it,
   its frets are the ear-rings of the widow with nine children.
I will cause Confucius's music-teacher, Master Tang, to play
   upon it the time-honoured melodies,
And Bo Ya will sing this song to it:

   'Among the thick ear-rings of wheat
      the wild cockerel flies at dawn.
   Facing the desolate village, alas,
      the bird turns its back on the withered ashtree.
   The paths and road are blocked, alas,
      I face the everflowing torrent.'

The birds will hear it,
   fold their wings and be unable to fly,
The wild beasts will hear it,
   droop their ears and be unable to walk,
The creeping ants and insects will hear it,
   cease their gnawing and be unable to move.
This song is the sum of the world's sadness:
   can the Prince force himself to rise and listen to it?'
The Prince said: 'I am ill,
   I am not yet well enough.'

*

The courtier said:
'Cook
  the flesh of a young calf
    garnished with the tenderest shoots,
Brew
  a harmonius broth from plump dogflesh,
    cap it with a layer of mountain truffles,
Prepare the rice of Chu
  and the fine cereals of the South,
    choice dainties,
Rolled into balls,
  dropped in the mouth,
    they will melt at a taste,
Summon the master chef Yi Yin to perform the cuisine,
  the famed cook Yi Ya will blend and spice it,
And then prepare well-cooked bear's paw,
  add a sweet sauce,
Take delicately sliced, braised lean meats,
  slivers of fresh carp,
Adorn the whole with autumn-yellow sapan,
  September mushrooms plucked amidst white dew,
Serve with wine steeped in orchids,
  a sip will freshen the mouth,
Then add the flesh of wild pheasant,
  the foetus of home-reared leopards,
Taste a little rice,
  drink much tin gruel,
And it will be like sun melting snow.
This is the sum of the world's cuisine:
  can the Prince force himself up to savour it?'
The Prince replied 'I am ill,
  I am not yet well enough.'

*

The courtier said: 'Bring fine horses of the Kingdom of Zhao,
  matched by age and harnessed to chariots,
The front span as swift as flying birds,
  the rear span as frisky as the heavenly gazelle.

Feed them a fine mash of wheat—
   their mettle will be without compare.
Caparisoned with stout harness and bit
   they will gallop the level roads.
Then have the horse-fancier Bo Lai
   to choose the order of the team,
Wang Liang and Cao Fu, as master-charioteers,
   brave Qin Que and stout Lou Ji to be outriders.
With men like these to control such fiery horses
   or right the toppled chariot,
Then you may lay wagers of a thousand talents,
   compete in races of a thousand miles.
These are the sum of the world's mettle—
   Can the Prince force himself up to mount his chariot?'
The Prince replied: "I am ill,
   I am not yet well enough.'

*

The courtier said: 'Ascend the pagoda of Jing Yi,
   to the south you will look out to Mount Jing
   to the north you will see the vast waters of Ru,
To the left the mighty Yang-tze,
   to the right Lake Dong-ting
   the world holds few such joys.
Then you may summon scholars learned in disputation
   who will in verse describe the mountains and rivers,
   exhaustively name each tree and plant,
All these they will marvellously classify—
   to make the Sum of Things.
After this brief excursion
   you will come down to feast and wine in Yu Huai Palace
   whose corridors are belvederes,
With storey upon storey painted dark green,
   interconnecting carriageways,
   sinuous ornamental ponds.
Amongst birds reared here is the white-striped Hun-zhang,
   the Eastern Egret, the Peacock, the Kun-gu Jungle Fowl,
   the Mandarin Duck, the Green Crested Grebe;

Some birds sport turquoise crests of kingfisher feather,
  others boast purple throat-bands;
The hornless Dragon-Fowl, the Virtuous Shepherd-Bird—
  their song harmonizes.
Endless varieties of fish leap and splash
  their fins strumming the waters.
By the fresh green rivulets grow
  elegant grasses and marsh-reeds,
The convolvulus and opulent water-lily,
  tender mulberry-bushes and river willows
  with white leaves and purple stems;
Mighty pine-trees and camphor laurels whose branches brush
    the heavens,
  the turpentine tree and the coir palm
  form forests as far as the eye can see.
Manifold thick fragrant shade blends with every sound of
    rustling
  the treetops are pliant to the wind,
  the foliage shifts from light to shadow.
Orator Jing Chun serves the drinks,
  Lutemaster Du Lien sees to the music.
Dainty foods are laid out,
  dishes of fish and fowl stand ready.
Exquisite colours charm the eye,
  fine sonorities delight the ear.
Then like a whirlwind the tunes of the South strike up:
  the melodies of lubricious Zheng and lascivious Wei
  float upon the air.
Then are summoned Lady Xi Shi, concubine Zheng Shu,
  Lady Sun-Pattern, Mistress Broken Stem,
  South Baby, Lu Zhou, Fu Yu and other lovely women
  trailing dresses of every colour,
  hair hanging like swallowtails,
  eyes provocative, bosoms hinting at
  dark permissiveness.
They bring water to bathe in,
  turmeric ungents perfume their naked bodies,
Their hair piled up like dust-clouds
  where floats the scent of orchids,

They slip on flimsy silks to await the lovemakers' couch.
This is the sum of the world's expansive luxury :
    can the Prince force himself up to dally?'
The Prince replied: 'I am ill,
    I am not yet well enough.'

*

The courtier said: 'Well then for you I would offer
    to break in steeds,
    harness them to panelled light chariots.
Mounted in a car drawn by noble stallions
    in your right hand you will grasp Prince Xia's quiver of
        straight arrows,
    in your left, the bow, crowblack, of the Yellow Emperor.
Then set out to Cloud-Dream Forest,
    drive through the Orchid Lowlands,
    halt by the Great River's flood,
    rest among the marsilea plants,
    swallow the transparent wind,
    get drunk on the sun's air,
    unshackle your spring heart,
Pursue the crafty beasts of the field,
    shoot down light-soaring birds,
Try out the talents of hound and horse,
    tire out the wild beasts' hoof,
    exhaust the charioteer, his skill,
Tiger and leopard flushed out of hiding will take fright,
    birds of prey will fly on wings of panic.
As the horse runs full tilt the harness-bells will tinkle;
    they will leap like fish, butt like stags.
You will tread deer and hare, trample down antelope.
    The beasts will sweat, cower, fall exhausted,
    they will die unscathed, of fright.
Your chariots in the rear will be piled with game.
The world knows no mightier hunt :
    can you force yourself to rise and join the meet?'
The Prince replied: 'I am ill,
    I am not yet well enough.'

But in his eyes glinted a livelier light,
  a happy look began to steal upon his majestic countenance.

*

Seeing the Prince's look of joy,
  the courtier developed his theme, and said:
'Night hunting fires will light up the heavens,
  war chariots roll like thunder,
The standards flutter aloft
  and feather-pennants crazy in array,
You will set the riders in hot pursuit;
  scenting the killed game,
  they will compete for first place.
The undergrowth will be beaten flat
  clear to the very frontiers.
A beast perfect in hide and pelt will later be sacrificed
  to your ancestors.'
Then came the Prince's interruption: 'Excellent.
  I should like to hear more of this.'

*

The courtier said: 'That is not all there is to it.
There, within the hazel forests, the deep marshlands,
  enveloped in dusk-smoke
  rhinoceros and tiger appear together,
Stout hunting warriors, fierce and steadfast,
  their sleeves rolled up to do battle,
White blades glinting like white rocks,
  a tangle of lances and spears all stabbing.
The bag's recorded, achievements written down,
  prizes of gold and silk awarded,
They roll out grass mats, spread couches,
  and for the chief sacrificer prepare a feast:
The finest wine, the choicest dishes,
  thin cuts well braised to banquet the retainers.
Such loyalty is a hardness
  firmer than iron or rock.
Loud they sing and tell of deeds,
  long life to the King, unwearying.

43

This is truly something you, my Prince, could delight in.
　Can you not force yourself up to join this venture?'
The Prince said: 'Indeed I would like to take part.
　It's just that I feel my presence a hindrance
　to the other lords.'
Yet nonetheless he took on colour.

*

The courtier said: 'Soon comes the eighth month, the fifteenth
　　day.
Then princes from far regions journey together with their
　　brothers
To look down at Guang-ling's mighty flood-bore.
Till now they have not seen the power of waves,
　even the looking bowls you over,
Seeing it rushing and rising,
　　tearing and pulling,
　　　rending and hurrying,
　　rearing together,
　　　pouring away.
Had you but the words to describe it,
　its shape would elude you like its curves.
O see it, fear it, be stunned by it, ground by it,
　sudden flusterer, roller and roysterer,
　　pouring forth, roaring away, massive in onslaught,
Swallowing up the Southern hills,
　evilly lusting for the Eastern sea,
A rainbow vaulting the blue skies,
　building a cliff in the mind,
It flows and roars without end,
　seeking a path to the Sun-mother's home.
Now up it drives and down it goes,
　No telling where its end,
The waves in confusion flow and tear,
　Clash suddenly and no return.
Look there at the Southern bank,
　rushing to the distance.

You are empty and filled with a violent fear,
    an impression of waves so deeply staining your heart
    it cannot be washed away.
But water refreshes the lungs,
    purges the bowels, cleanses the hands and feet,
        soaks the teeth and hair,
Drives away languid humours,
    cleans off all dust and dirt,
Makes certain uncertainties,
    rinses the ears and eyes.
Suppose now there was some despondency,
Why, even the hunchback would straighten up,
    the cripple walk,
The deaf would hear, the blind would be enlightened
    to gaze upon this scene.
How much more for those with but light afflictions,
    disciples of wine, hangover-sick.
As it is said of old, Truly no words of mine
    could make a sum of this enlightenment.'
The Prince said: 'Excellent.
    Yet what is the nature of this flood?'

*

The courtier said: 'It is not recorded.
    Yet I have heard my teacher say
        the water possesses three things
    that spirits lack:
Sudden thunder heard from a hundred miles;
    the sea-bore flowing back against itself,
        blanketing mountains in the cloud
    endlessly day and night;
Slowly it starts, gathering speed
    till the ominous swell of waves
        builds up a mighty rhythm
  like the Eastern egret soaring,
Advancing and tipped with small white crests
        as bright
    as the silken parasols of white chariots
        driven by white horses.

Then the chasers become cloud-confused,
　　rushing forward like a full-geared army
With small waves hurrying lightly—
　　generals on the wing riding light chariots.
A team of six dragons pulling Tai Bo the water spirit's car
　　a massing perspective of rainbows together,
　　　　pressing ahead,
High and high, low and low,
　　forward and back hustling and crowding,
Now like a castellated fort,
　　now like a cavalry and footsoldiers forward advancing,
Its noise is a roaring, it fills the sky with seething,
　　its strength cannot be withstood.
See the two banks, massive flood-anger around them,
　　for a moment dark and lowering,
　　suddenly then it's palpable,
　　to overwhelm, to undermine,
The waves like brave soldiers
　　forward rushing without fear,
　　smashing down walls and stopping breaches,
It roars round curves, leaps over sandbanks,
　　those it meets die, those who oppose are smashed,
Gathers up speed to thunder past Huo Wei Ford,
　　with a fearful rush it fills the valleys,
Its maelstrom whirls round Qing Mie
　　laying a muffled ambush for Tan Huan Forest,
Descending on Mount Wu Ze
　　for the assault on Bone-Mother Battlefield,
It cuts Red Crag away, sweeps past Purple Mulberry Grove,
　　its advance is impetuous thunder.
Truly it robs warriors of spirit
　　in its enraged vibration,
　　In its gulping and gurgling, the strength of galloping horses,
　　in its swirling and swallowing, the sound of hungry
　　　　　　　　　　　　　　drum-thunder.
Clear rising, the back waves leap clear over,
　　follow up to do battle at the mouth of Ji Ji River.
Fish are stranded, beasts cannot run, birds cannot fly,
　　they flap their wings, winged waves like clouds.

It violates the Southern Mountain,
    steals up to attack the Northern shore,
Tearing down dykes, flattening the Western Weir,
In dangerous sport it playfully swallows reservoirs,
    victory alone will check it,
But the quick advance of the gurgling flood
    rips out everything with its mighty waves.
This is the sum of cruelty,
    fish and turtle are helpless, tossed and turned, floating and
                                    bloated, stranded,
Even the spirits would be afeared:
    so many abilities baffling speech
That men fall down in fright,
    faint from fear,
    slowly to regain consciousness.
This is the world's most varied, strange and terrible vista:
    can the Prince not force himself up to look at it?'
The Prince said: 'I am ill,
    I am not yet well enough.'

                        *

The courtier said: 'Then let me summon
    men of skill and knowledge,
Schooled in policy and debate:
    Master Zhuang Zi the Taoist,
    Yang Zi the Individualist,
    Mo Di the Chivalrous Altruist,
    Bien Zhuan, Zhan He and others,
To expound to you the nature of the world,
    reason out the rights and wrongs of Manifold Existence,
Confucius and Lao-Zi could test and observe,
    Mencius could investigate and assess,
    out of ten thousand wisdoms
    not one would be lacking:
Such is the sum of succinct words and excellent teaching:
    why not listen, my Prince?'

The Prince heaved himself up with both hands,
    saying:
    'Things are clear, it is as if
    I hear the wise disputers' words.'
His fever broke
    and in a sweat
Suddenly
    his sickness had ended.

Mei Sheng

The Prose-Poem of the Beautiful Person

Handsome Si-ma Xiang-ru was at leisure in the Capital. He had journeyed to see the Prince of Liang, who delighted in his conversation. But Zhou Yang vilified him to the Prince, saying: 'True it is that Xiang-ru is a fine figure of a man. But despite his elegant dress, his noble features, there is deceit and disloyalty in his good looks and he uses his flattering command of rhetoric to achieve pleasure. He has been wandering about the seraglio of Your Highness. I wonder if you have noticed this?' The Prince asked Xiang-ru: 'Are you addicted to lust?' 'I am not,' he replied. Then the Prince said: 'Well, you must be like Confucius and Mo Di.' But Xiang-ru answered: 'Those ancients avoided all acquaintance with sensual delights. The like of Confucius and Mo Di had only to hear of a beautiful woman and they made themselves scarce. If they heard a woman of the palace singing in the distance, they would turn their chariots around. It was as if they considered women as dangerous as raging fire and deep water, and hid away from them on secluded mountains. Seeing they found no opportunity for temptation, how can we be sure that they were not libertines?'

When I was young
　　long years in the West
　　　　I dwelt by myself in a solitary place.
My mansion was vast and rambling,
　　yet I found no diversions.
My neighbour to the East had a daughter
　　black her hair, comely her figure,
　　　　moth eyebrows and white teeth,
Features full and sensual,
　　a lustre like flashing light.
She often gazed towards my residence
　　as if she would wish me to join her;
As she mounted her steps
　　she would pause and look at me.

Though I lived there three years
   I avoided her and never complied,
      for I was mindful of Your Highness's
              strict standards:
      you had commanded me to ride eastwards.
My journey took me through lascivious Zheng and lubricious
   Wei,
      my path took me through Sang Zhong.
In the morning I set off from the region of Zhun Wei,
      in the evening I lodged at a great mansion.
This mansion was an empty but elegant residence
     all by itself among the clouds:
       its doors had been shut to the light,
         it seemed a fairy palace.
I pushed my way in through the shuttered door,
     found my way to the hall;
Exotic perfumes and fine scents hovered in the air,
     rich screens and tapestries furnished it.
And there in this room a lady waited alone:
     curvaciously beautiful, reclining on the bed
In sweetly perfumed and languid charm,
     her skin clear, her features vivid.
Seeing hesitation in my step,
     she smiled and said:
'Sir, what country are you from?
   Have you travelled far to this place?'
She offered me wine,
     brought out a bird-toned lute;
So I touched the strings
   and played White Snow
     and the Dark Orchid.
And then she sang this poem:
     'In solitude here, alas,
       in empty vastness, no-one to care for me,
     I long for my handsome prince, alas,
       I am wounded with sorrow.
     Here is my handsome prince, alas,
       but how long he delays,

Till day becomes evening, alas,
    and my flower complexion fades.
To you I dare confide my body,
    long may you and I be intimate.'
She was so close that her jade hairpins
  brushed my hat,
    her gauze sleeves whispered against my clothes.
The sun went down in the West,
  mysterious dusk set in,
    the light was swallowed up.
Outside, the wind flowed sad and chill,
  cold silk snow swirling.
In our closed room all was quiet,
  not a sound was heard.
On the bed were laid
  exotic coverlets and sheets.
A golden brazier breathed out scented smoke,
    the curtains round the bed were lowered,
The quilt turned back,
  the ivory pillow set horizontal.
She stepped out of her robe,
  showed off her undergarments,
Revealed her white body,
  full delicate nakedness,
    shapely beauty.
Then she came close to me
  wrapping her soft body
    slipping like paste around me.
My pulse of course was regular,
  my heart was purposeful within my breast:
As the Odes say:
  'Clearly we were sworn to good faith':
  I held my resolution upright,
    there could be no faltering.
With such lofty example I made my long goodbye.

Si-ma Xiang-ru

Prose-Poem to the Goddess of the River Luo

In the third year of our present Emperor's reign, I was return-
ing from an audience at the capital about to ford the waters
of the Luo. The ancients have told us that a goddess dwelt
there whom they called the fairy concubine Mi. Mindful of
what the poet Song Yu relates of the affair between the fairy
and the King of Chu, accordingly I wrote this poem. And here
I set down the words:

*

From the regions of the capital
   I was returning to my Eastern fief.
I circumvented Mount Yi Que
   traversed the Sunder-Axle Pass,
The length of Tong Valley
   surmounting the Peak of Jing.
Then it was the sun slanted Westward,
   my chariot groaned, the horses were weary
So I had them unharnessed amidst the ambrosial grasses of the
     marsh,
   pastured my team in those purple fields,
For being hesitant to penetrate the Forests of Yang
   my eyes chanced to linger upon the waters of Luo.

*

My spirit was moved, my soul was startled,
   and suddenly my thoughts fled abroad.
Looking down into those depths I still saw nothing,
   looking up it was the strangest prospect.
For there I perceived a beautiful woman
   standing upon the desolate shore.

*

I plucked at my charioteer's sleeve
   and these words I uttered:

'Do you have eyes to see that person yonder?
   What lady is she? such is her beauty.'
He answered me: 'Your servant has heard of the fairy of Luo
         River:
   they call her the concubine Mi.
Yet she whom you see, my lord,
      can it be that lady?
   How is her appearance?
      Your servant longs to hear.'

                    *

This is what I told him:
'Such is her appearance:
   she rises like a startled swan
      as undulating as the playful water-snake.
In clear glory she surpasses the chrysanthemum in autumn
   her features a pine in the spring.
O presence hardly perceived, cloud feathers enveloping the
         moon,
   ruffled, stirred like swirling snows
      in the wind's current.
From a distance I gaze upon her
   bright like the sun climbing the dawn-clouds,
When I approach to observe her
   her radiance is the transient ripples round the water-lily.

                    *

In figure she is the golden mean
   in stature she complies with the measure,
Her shoulders are as gently sloping hills
   her waist a slender band of white silk.
When she raises her head, her exquisite breasts
   the white snow of their flesh is exposed.
A black mount her piled coiffure,
   elegant eyebrows delicately curving,
Cinnabar lips just pouting
   yet revealing a gleam of her white teeth,
From her lovely eyes a gracious look,
   the dimples in her cheeks are all-commanding.

Strange elegance her carriage, piquant modesty
  calm features composed with a body compliant,
That curvaceous posture,
  that beauty almost articulate.
Wondrously clothed, surpassing all other ages,
  the echo of a painting,
She shifts the shimmering pearls of her light dress.
  In her ears are pendants of fabled jade.
In her hair are kingfisher hairpins, gold-embossed,
  matching the jewels that set off her body.
She wears the embroidered shoes of a distant region,
  she trails a petticoat of mist-silk.
O that lingering perfume of strange orchids,
  as her little feet tread gently at the mountain's corner.'

*

Sudenly she released her body
  to wander and dance most playfully,
In the left hand fluttering a strange fan
  in the right hand a sprig of cool cassia.
O she waved her white wrists amidst those spirit marshes
  plucking at mysterious ambrosia by the swirling waters.
My emotions delight in her gentle loveliness
  my heart is in a turmoil and I am most confused.
O where is the good matchmaker to unite our joy?
  We rely on words exchanged over the rippling waves.
We long to express our white silk emotion,
  and I would loosen her jade waist-belt to play with her.
Alas for my beauty's inner feelings;
  perhaps she practises the 'Rites and Rules'
    and is familiar with the 'Odes'
O but she lifts those jade waist-pendants to unite with me,
  beckoning over the deep waters
    inviting me to the tryst.
Indeed her physical form is real, sincere,
  but I fear she is a spirit tricking me,
Being mindful of how one Zhou Fu was similarly beguiled;
  O how I sorrow at my own doubt and suspicion.

I clothe my face with the smile of a mind composed,
   I hold myself in check.

*

At this the water-sprite senses what I feel,
   she is hesitant, she is confused;
Her spirit lustre flickers uncertain
   between happy light and sad darkness;
Her little body shudders like a hesitant crane
   as if she would fly away but does not wish to fly;
She treads scented pastures,
   her steps scatter the fabled flowers;
O but loudly she sings her eternal longing,
   her voice of sadness bitterly protracted.

*

Then suddenly see there came a host of strange spirits
   summoned as companions to play with her
Some there are who sport in the clear water
   others soar over the spirit islets
Others still pluck bright pearls
   and some cull kingfisher feathers
And the two fairies of the Xiang River from the South
   leading the Playful Girl from the banks of the Han.
O they sigh that like the Bitter Gourd Star
   for my lady there'll be no partner,
They sing of the separation of the Spinning Maid
   and the Ploughboy
   each in their remote regions of the sky.
She lifts her body's beauty,
   hiding behind her long sleeves she gazes once more at me.

*

That little body soon will become the fast-flying wild duck
   though she remains now a spirit still hesitant.
Slowly she treads over the waves
   and on the water leaves a trace of her satined feet.
To her movement there is no regular pattern,
   sometimes fearful, sometimes resigned,

It is a progress difficult to predict:
    she must go yet she would stay.
She turns those eyes full of a brightness
    illumining her jade countenance,
She has words for me yet she cannot say them,
    her pneuma is that of the dark orchid,
O those flower features so alluring
    I have long forgotten all thought of nourishment.

*

Then the god of the elements calls in his winds,
    the goddess of rivers stills her waves,
Ping Yi the river god sounds his drums,
    Fairy Nu Wa plays her shrill pipes,
Up soar the flying fishes ready to depart,
    the phoenix bells tinkle for the retinue will leave together
Six dragons, their countenance majestic, are harnessed in a
        team,
    they bear the cloud chariot soaring and dipping,
Leviathan and his mate leap to each side of the carriage,
    the beasts of the river serve as bodyguards.

*

Then they pass away over those northern river-lands
    beyond the southern ridge.
She turns her white neck
    she strains her clear eyes,
Those crimson lips move to utter gentle words
    telling me how lovers' meetings are spun
        in fate's great web:
'O sad it is the ways of men and spirits remain so different,
    hateful too that ours was no meeting
        ordained when we were younger!'
She raises her silk sleeves to wipe her eyes
    but the flowing tears wet her breasts.
'I weep that our happy union is forever broken,
    I sorrow that once gone I shall be in a
        different place.

I have but a small token to show my love for you,
  I offer you this bright ear-ring from the
    Southern River.
Though I shall be hidden away in the region of the fairies,
  my lord, this token of my heart will be for ever with you.'
Then suddenly I no longer knew where she was.
  I sorrowed that the mist had blotted out her light.

*

So it was that I turned my back on those low-lying lands,
  meaning to ascend to the high ridge,
Though my feet moved forward,
  my spirit lagged behind.
I thought of her little love-token
  only to look around and embrace sorrow.
O I longed that her spirit body should again appear,
  but I embarked in my light boat to journey upstream.
Slowly it floated on the long waters forgetting the way home.
  The more I thought of her the more my longing grew.
Troubled all night, I could not sleep,
  but braving the manifold frosts I reached the dawn.
I summoned my servant to yoke up the team,
  ours was an eastward journey home.
He held the bridle, he cracked the whip,
  but sadly I hesitated nor could I yet set out.

Cao Zhi

III. The Three Kingdoms
A.D. 220-280

The Three Kingdoms

With the collapse of the Later Han Dynasty, China was plunged into a period of internecine turmoil. Though there were short-lived dynasties which supplied some form of political stability, like the Jin (A.D. 265–419) for many years the country was divided into two rival political entities, the North and the South. The northern area had been subjected to barbarian incursions. Though the so-called barbarians rapidly underwent a process of sinification and adopted Chinese culture and governmental institutions so that we must look upon them as something quite different from the Vandals or Goths, this whole period from the collapse of the Han to the establishment of the Tang in A.D. 618 can be considered an interim stage in the history of Chinese civilization. China resembled an enormous cooking pot into which all sorts of strange ingredients had been tossed—Chinese meat with foreign spices and herbs (e.g., Buddhism and Central Asiatic cultures)—to remain bubbling and seething until the glorious Tang emerged.

It is not surprising that the literature of the last years of the dying Han and of the Three Kingdoms immediately following it, reflects many conflicting values—on the one hand a desire by the more socially conscious intellectual such as Chen Lin to identify himself with the sufferings of the common man in times of war and famine, and on the other a fatalistic almost Taoist cynicism seen in the disillusionment of the politician Cao Cao when he realizes the hopelessness of his own noble ambitions. Both the words of General Cao Cao and Chen Lin's common soldier, though manifestly different in experience, mirror a common despair born of the same age. Gone for good is the confidence of the courtly Han prose-poem. The great proto-realist poets of this period rejected the *fu*, born of the romantic *Songs of The South*, and emasculated by stereotyped intellectualism, but envigorated their verse by choosing as their models the simple folk song of the Han (the *yue-fu*); these poems were composed to a regular number of words (five, seven and sometimes four) to a line, often based on old popular tunes and melodies. In the folk song of the *Shi Jing* and *yue-fu* there was an austerity of sentiment which always appealed to both the demands of functionalist verse, and the rustic, often, stoical Taoist poets.

Cao Cao (Martial Emperor of Wei. A.D. 155–220)

Warlord, poet, and usurper, given to fits of uncontrollable rage; for centuries he has incurred the opprobrium of his fellow countrymen. In fiction and drama he has been personified as the embodiment of treachery and cunning, one who could certainly 'put the murderous Machiavel to school'. It has taken the Marxist historians of Communist China in the fifties to present us with a fairer appraisal of both the man and his achievements. The poor fellow's temper is best explained by terrible headaches resulting from a fatal brain tumour—granted he had his court physician, the talented Hua Tuo, imprisoned and poisoned for daring to offer to trepan him. He was a great poet who displayed a surprising degree of sensitivity—at times he even identified himself with his suffering troops, forgetting that it was his own ambition which exhausted them on his notorious forced marches. The speed at which he moved his men from one military objective to another has given rise to the still current Chinese equivalent of 'talk of the devil'—'*Shuo dao Cao Cao, Cao Cao jiu dao*'. 'If you talk of Cao Cao, he'll turn up'.

Dr Jerome Chen, in his excellent biography of Mao, *Mao and the Chinese Revolution*, has juxtaposed part of his and Michael Bullock's translation of part of the poem on p. 62 with a poem by Chairman Mao. The two great men have much in common—history has still not passed final judgment on either. Perhaps it never will.

Chen Lin (?—died A.D. 217)

During the wars of the great rival warlords following Dong Zhuo's rebellion in A.D. 189, Chen Lin served as a secretary to Yuan Shao. Later he went over to Yuan's opponent, Cao Cao.

Along with Cao Cao and his three sons seven other great poets are traditionally linked with this period; these seven are known as the *Jian-An Qi-Zi*, Seven Great Masters of the Jian An Reign Period (A.D. 196–220). One of them was Chen Lin.

Chen Lin has written the poem on p. 63 in the earlier folk song style of *yue-fu*, basing it on the title of a particular old melody popular a couple of hundred or more years previously. By describing the conscripts building the Great Wall hundreds of years before his own time, Chen Lin is giving a precedent to later Chinese writers of functional or satirical verse. His setting is historical but his message (the horrors of war, conscription, corvée, etc.) has a contemporary reference.

Such precautions were obviously necessary for a writer living in the shadow of the ruthless Cao Cao. During the Tang, Bo Ju-yi was one of many poets who adopted the same safety measures.

Bibliography

Frodsham, J. D., trans. and annot., (with the collaboration of Ch'eng Hsi), *An Anthology of Chinese Verse*, Oxford University Press, London 1967.

The existence of this fine collection covering the work of poets from the Han right up to the establishment of the Sui Dynasty (A.D. 581) explains why this period is hardly represented at all in this book. Dr Frodsham's first poem is the anonymous ballad on the title of which Chen Lin based this poem.

'Fabled Tortoise – Long Living'

Fabled tortoise—long living
Yet his span is set,
Mighty basilisk—cloud soaring
Must end in dust and ashes,
Old steed in paddock grazing
Yearning for long past races,
Stout hero in his twilight years
His resolution knows no ending,
Success and failure, now up now down
For each there comes a time,
Nor does this rest alone with heaven
So foster delight—nurture pleasure,
And you may live for ever.

Cao Cao

Somewhere on the Great Wall

At a breach in the Wall they water the horses,
So cold it cuts to the bone.
To the sergeant-at-arms a soldier says:
'We're conscripts from the Plains, no right to keep us!'
—'There's a job here and you're going to do it,
Just swing that spade, keep singing with the rest!'
—'We'd rather die fighting
Than rot away minding the Wall.'
Like a mighty chain is the Great Wall
link after link three thousand miles in all.
On this stretch there's many a young lad
And of widows at home just the same number.
In a letter to his wife one soldier wrote:
'Better marry again, don't wait for me!
Be good to your new in-laws and
Now and then spare a thought for your old man.'
To the frontier came this reply:
'Why do you talk so unkind to me?'
—'I'm up to my neck in danger here,
No point in keeping my bed warm.
If you get a son don't take any trouble,
but a girl, well, nothing but the best for her,
You've never seen this side of the Wall,
Bodies and bones lying six feet deep.'
—'Since I was young and betrothed
I've always cared for you.
Well I can guess the horror of the front
But that's no reason for thinking just of me.'

Chen Lin

IV. The Tang Dynasty
A.D. 618-907

The Tang Dynasty

The Tang was the golden age of Chinese classical culture. Poetry received a tremendous impetus from the establishment of the competitive examination system of entry into the governmental hierarchy. It has been said 'the Tang obtained officials (*shi*) by poems (*shi*)'. This pithy pun may be a simplification but certainly the *ke-ju* or selection by examination favoured the fostering of an élite 'club' of literary men. *The Quan Tang Shi* or *Anthology of Tang Verse* compiled as late as the eighteenth century when many of the originals were already lost, contains some 48,900 poems written by no less than 2,300 poets.

When we talk of poetry throughout this period we refer primarily to *shi* or 'regular verse'. The years immediately preceding witnessed important discoveries in the field of phonetics; Shen Yue's (A.D. 441–513) study of the tonal structure of the language pointed the way for the creation of new patterns in prosody during the early Tang. Chief amongst the new verse are the 'end stop quatrain' (*jue-ju*) and the poem in cadenced metre (*lü-shi*). In such forms abounding in metrical subtleties, antithesis and parallelism the Tang poet, often living an ordered life closely knitted to the complex needs of official duty, can be said in his literary stance to anticipate Eliot's in the sense that for him 'freedom was only freedom when it appeared against the background of an artificial limitation'. Of course it is equally true that he could always 'feel easy in his harness', and when the narrative exposition of social maladies was called for we find not only

Bo Ju-yi and Yuan Zhen, but even Du Fu falling back on the older and less restrictive ballad forms, though never because they wished 'to play tennis without the net'.

Li Bo (A.D. 701–762)

Li Bo or Li Tai-bo remains the most popular, perhaps the greatest, of China's poets. The universality of his artistry mirrors the many facets of his character. Solitary mystic, heroic romantic, drunken bravo, Li Bo was all these and many more. No other literary figure in China fulfils the ideals of bohemian *sprezzatura* so completely as Li Bo.

Bibliography

Waley, Arthur, *The Poetry and Career of Li Bo*, Allen and Unwin, London, 1950.

Shigeyoshi Obata, *The Works of Li Bo the Chinese Poet*, Paragon Reprints, New York, 1965.

Wang Wei (A.D. 701–761)

A poet, painter and musician Wang Wei is one of China's most protean genii. Though not without its ups and downs he enjoyed, unlike his contemporary Li Bo, a fairly distinguished official career. When twenty-one he was made Da Yue Cheng or kapellmeister at the great Emperor Ming Huang's court.

It is particularly in the realm of painting that his impact on later generations was most felt. He is said to have been the innovator of the *xuan-ran* or wash technique in water colour painting and to have developed the use of atmospheric perspective. A beautiful fourteenth-century copy by Zhao Meng-fu of Wang's famous twenty-three-foot panoramic scroll *Scenes of the Felloe River* or *Wang Chuan tu* can be seen in the British Museum.

Of this great creative spirit of China's golden age it has been said: 'In his painting there is poetry, in his poetry there is painting.'

Bibliography

Chang Yin-nan and Walmsley, Lewis C., *The Poems of Wang Wei*, Charles E. Tuttle, Rutland, Vermont, 1958.

Walmsley, L. C. and D. B., *Wang Wei, The Painter-Poet*, Charles E. Tuttle, Rutland, Vermont, 1968.

Du Fu (A.D. 712–770)

Although a lifelong friend of Li Bo, this reserved and honest official was totally different in both temperament and career. Du Fu was the epitome of Confucian integrity, and many consider him as great a poet as his rumbustious contemporary.

'The Sergeant at Tong Pass' is one of a poetic triptych *The Three Minor Officials* or *San Li* inspired by the catastrophic civil wars following the revolt of the barbarian soldier An Lu-shan in December A.D. 755. Du Fu was deeply involved in the tragedy of these events. In Bo Ju-yi's letter to Yuan Zhen in which he outlines his theories on realistic satirical verse, Bo considers *The Three Minor Officials* one of only thirty-odd poems of Du Fu where he realizes the satirical ideal —the rest he dismisses. Though we can ignore this totally unfair judgment, it is obvious why 'The Sergeant of Tong Pass' should have appealed to Bo Ju-yi.

Bibliography

Hawkes, David, *A Little Primer of Tu Fu*, Oxford University Press, 1967. (Offers a magnificent insight into Du Fu's life and career seen through his verse. Thirty-five poems are analysed with the original Chinese text, a word-for-word translation, plus an exhaustive exegesis and final polished version.)

Hung, William, *Tu Fu*, Harvard University Press, Cambridge, Mass., 1952.

Zhang Ji (A.D. 768–830)

Friend and advisor to Bo Ju-yi he was a great influence on the latter's didactic ballads, and not surprisingly wins an honourable mention in Bo's famous Letter to Yuan Zhen. Like Bo Ju-yi he was plagued by bad eyesight and though he passed his Literary Examination in 799 he lived in relative poverty and obscurity until eight years before his death when he was made Second Secretary of the Water Board.

In China the tiger is King in the animal world. Though open to interpretation the poem on p. 76 is probably allegorical in nature, inspired, no doubt, by the classical adage '*Ke-zheng meng yu hu*'—'tyrannical governments surpass the tiger in savagery'.

Bo Ju-yi (A.D. 772–846)

Together with his friend Yuan Zhen, Bo complemented in verse the great Confucian revival championed by Han Yu (768–824) in prose.

To him the poet was to be the dedicated spokesman for the sufferings of the inarticulate peasantry, an outspoken critic of the excesses of knavish politicians. The colloquial vigour of his verse reflects the unbending sincerity of its writer, and there is never anything priggish about his moral purpose. In his famous letter to Yuan Zhen he tells us that once whilst relaxing in an inn he was delighted to notice that a sing-song girl recognized him as the author of two well-known ballads. Popular acclaim from such lowly elements undoubtedly meant more to the modest poet than the plaudits of the exalted, for he goes on to say '*Ming shi gong-qi, bu ke duoqu*'—'fame is a public commodity of which no one man has a monopoly'.

Bibliography

Waley, Arthur, *The Life and Times of Po Chü-i*, Allen and Unwin, London, 1947. (This study of the poet and his background is as comprehensive as could be wished.)

Yuan Zhen (A.D. 779–831)

In many Chinese literary histories you will find the author referring to the verse of Yuan-Bo—after reading a few sentences it will become apparent to even the uninitiated that this composite individual is in reality the two poets, Yuan Zhen and Bo Ju-yi. It is indeed difficult to speak of one without the other. They were intimate friends and shared the same aims and ideals. Of the two, Yuan is slightly more difficult to read in Chinese. He often lacks the simple clarity of his friend, and is prone to more frequent classical reference, but this does little to detract from the beauty of his poetry. Yuan Zhen and Bo Ju-yi's brother, Bo Xing-jian, were accomplished short-story writers. (See Cyril Birch and D. Keene (eds.), *Anthology of Chinese Literature*, Penguin Books, Harmondsworth, 1967, pp. 301–23.)

Zhang Jie (born A.D. 837–?)

Little is known of this poet. One Chinese commentator tells us, 'after repeated unsuccessful attempts to pass his doctoral examination he became a wanderer. Nobody knows what happened to him in the end.' Amongst Chinese poets, this is a common-enough story.

Chen Yu-lan (late ninth–early tenth century)

China has produced a number of female poets—and Chen Yu-lan is one of them. She was married to Wang Jia, one of the better known poets of the late Tang.

Wei Zhuang (A.D. 836–910)

He is particularly remembered for his fine love poetry—most of which was written in the irregular *ci* form. Wei lived in the troubled last years of the Tang. Whilst he was in Chang An taking the official examinations he was trapped in the city when it was captured by Huang Chao's rebels. Some years later he wrote a long narrative poem vividly describing the calamitous events he had witnessed at first hand.

Luo Yin (A.D. 833–909)

A noted satirist whose scurrilous essays brought him into disrepute, and though talented, he repeatedly failed his examinations. This explains his bitter resentment against the effete court of Emperor Xi Zong.

When the Emperor fled from Chang An during Huang Chao's rebellion, he was accompanied by a motley crew of jugglers and entertainers. The antics of the chimps belonging to one of this bizarre retinue so delighted the Emperor that he conferred official honours on the trainer.

Seeing off the Archivist Li Yun
at Xie Tiao's Pavilion

Let them go, then, those yesterdays that can't be stopped
What worries me is that today's days are so vexatious
The long wind ten thousand miles blows the autumn wild
　　geese on
And viewing this let's get drunk in some upstairs room
'So you're an archivist? but you've got the marrow of the
　　old poets
A style, lively for the moderns
Together we'll hug enthusiasm and get some noble thoughts
　　flying
Why not climb up to the blue skies and grab the bright moon
　　by the horns?'
Draw a knife, cut the water, the water flows on quicker
Lift a glass, drown your sorrow, sorrow doubles sorrow.
Life in this world never measures up
So tomorrow let down your hair, float away with your boat.

Li Bo

'Her Presence Was a Roomful of Flowers'

Her presence was a roomful of flowers
Her absence is an empty bed
The brocade coverlet rolled up, unslept in
But the perfume left three years ago still lingers.
Though the scent remains
In person she'll not come again.
A love that is yellow leaves falling
Or white dew wet on the green moss.

Li Bo

Lament for the Old Master-Brewer of Xuan-Cheng

You're down below in the land of the yellow springs, old man,
No doubt still making that Old Spring brew.
As yet I'm not patronizing the Night Terrace,
So who will you find to sell your wine to now?

Li Bo

'Three Thousand Feet of Sorrow'

Three thousand feet of sorrow
Is the length of my white hair
But how I got this autumn frost
No bright mirror will explain.

Li Bo

To His Wife

Three hundred and sixty-five days
And every day I'm drunk as mud
What difference in being Li Bo's wife
Or married to old Commissioner Flask?

Li Bo

'Clear the Autumn Wind'

Clear the autumn wind
  Bright the autumn moon
Scurrying leaves gather
  to scatter once more
Cold crow perching
  startles again
Thinking together of being together
  who knows when
This time, this night
  such love is difficult to bear.

Li Bo

For a Lady I Met on the Road

Proudly steps the thoroughbred horse treading the fallen
  flowers,
The curving whip guides straight her fairy chariot.
Smiling the beauty lifts the pearled curtain,
Waving she points out a private door: 'That's my place.'

Li Bo

Viewing the Hunt

Muscle of wind, the horned bow twangs,
The commander is hunting by Wei River City.
The grass is wilted, sharp darts the falcon's eye,
The snows have melted, light run the horses' hoofs.

They are suddenly past Xin Feng,
Homeward to Xi Liu Garrison.
Glance back to where the shot kite falls:
A thousand level miles of evening cloud.

Wang Wei

The Sergeant at Tong Pass

They're digging in hard
Along the Tong Pass Road,
Steel nothing like as strong as the outer bastion,
Ten thousand feet or more the support trenches.
I ask the sergeant in charge:
'Doing all these repairs, will it keep off the Hun?'
He invited me down from my horse, showed me each corner
    and redoubt:
'They stretch like clouds these cavalry traps,
A bird on the wing couldn't get over them.
If the Hun comes we just hold on here,
You in the Capital have nothing to fear.
Just you look at them tricky points, sir,
Only wide enough for one at a time.
No room here for push of pike,
One of our lads in the gap, and he'll hold them off,
    that's always been the case.'

Alas for that battle at Peach Grove:
A thousand soldiers panicked and became fish in the river.
I beg you generals at the Pass,
Don't make the same mistake as General Ge-shu Han.

Du Fu

The Song of the Savage Tiger

Dark are the mountain forests to north and south
The savage tiger prowls in daylight around the village
At dusk he appears in person on the highways looking for food
And the mountain deer and antelope hold their breath
Yearly he bears his offspring in the deserted valleys
Male and female, big and small, there's no telling
Near his mountain lair is a little village
And often from the farmers there he'll steal a newborn calf
The local youths don't dare to shoot at him
In the forest helplessly they stare at his tracks

Zhang Ji

The Salt-Merchant's Wife

Salt-merchant's wife, you've stacks of gold and salt
That's not from your work in the corn or tending mulberries.
To South, North, East and West, there's nothing you lack,
For lucky wind and water is your domain, the boat's your
    mansion.
Once you were just a poor girl from Yang Zhou;
You married a great merchant from Xi Jiang
Your black silk hair hung low:
    now it's a mass of golden hairpins.
Your white wrists have grown plump,
    your silver bracelets pinch.
Now you yell at old retainers,
    now you upbraid the servant-girls.
I ask you, where does it all come from?
These fifteen years, your bridegroom has been a salt-merchant,
Not answerable to province or district, enjoying
    Imperial favour.
Each year the profits from salt should go to the government,
But little ends in the official chests, much in your own.
The Gabelle is lean, your household's in the fat;
The Monopolies Commission has no inkling, it's a long way
    away.
It's a long way too, isn't it,
    from the poor girl's diet of millet and fish,
The braised meats, oranges, fragrant rice that now you eat?
Stuffed full, powdered and painted,
    you doze in an upstairs room:
Those two red cheeks are really blossoming.
Merchant's wife, what luck to marry into salt,
With every morning, all day long, fine food to eat,
And every year, good clothes to wear—
But better not ask where it all comes from.
Well might we regret the passing of honest ministers.
Though incorruptibles are long since dead,
The past has no monopoly on them:
    today might turn up one or two.

Bo Ju-yi

The Barbarian Dancing-Girl

Foreign dancer, foreign dancer,
Your heart echoes the strings,
   your hands echo the drums;
As the tune strikes up, you raise your two sleeves high.
Snow swirling in a wind, your body
   a swaying flower in a storm,
Tireless you circle to the left, you twist to the right,
A thousand twists, ten thousand endless turns.
Nobody, nothing can match you,
The spinning chariot-wheel is slow, the whirlwind tardy.
When the music stops
   you curtsey to the Emperor;
The Emperor graces you with a brief smile.
O Barbarian turning girl who came from Ferghana,
In vain the hard journey East three thousand miles:
Here in China we're well supplied with foreign twisters:
How can you match their competence?
When the Tien Bao Rebellion threatened,
Ministers and concubines soon learned to turn full circle.
In the Palace was Lady Gui Fei,
Outside was young An Lu-shan,
Both adept in barbarian twisting.
In the Pear-Blossom Garden she was counted a concubine,
Below the Golden Cockerel Throne, he was adopted as a son.
An Lu-shan's barbarian turnings dazzled the Emperor's eyes.
To the regions beyond the Yellow River,
   War came unexpected.
Lady Gui Fei's foreign twist pleased His Majesty's heart.
She died rejected at Horse Ridge,
   but her memory haunts us still.
The affairs of state, after this, turned full circle.
These past fifty years it's been the same: a Court corrupted.
Little foreign circling girl, put purpose in your dance:
Just sing this song from time to time to enlighten the
   Emperor's ear.

Bo Ju-yi

Against Superstition

Vast the sea, stretching beyond, unfathomed, frontierless,
Over the cloudy swell, the smoky waves, in the deepest place
Tradition tells us rise the islands of the blest;
There on those mountains plentifully grows the elixir of life,
Whoever tastes becomes immortal.
Such talk gained credence from Ch'in's First Emperor, Han's
    Martial Ruler,
Yearly for them, alchemists sought exotic plants,
But of fairyland, the name is all we've ever heard,
And in the smoky wastes of water no such place was found.
Vast the sea, strong the winds,
Their eyes glimpsed no immortal isles,
And so they never dared return.
Many expeditions of boys and girls went out.
They grew old in the boat.
For royalty, deluded ministers hatch the most preposterous
    schemes.
In vain are prayers to God on high, the Lord Creator.
Just look, sir, see the Emperor's grave,
The Martial Ruler's burial mound,
All they achieved in the end was a sad wind
Blowing the grass on their tombs.
Remember too
The Tao Te Ching's five thousand words
Contain no mention of elixirs, not one word about immortals.
Lao Zi promised no ascent to heaven in broad daylight.

Bo Ju-yi

The Parrot

All day long chatter is interspersed with silence,
But at dead of night he startles from his rest.
Bright plumage is the reason he is captive,
Clarity of colour is his heart's regret.
At evening he pines for his bygone nest,
Often in spring he recalls the cry of his mate.
Yet anyone could open up his cage
And restore him to liberty of flight and call.

Bo Ju-yi

'To the East they Brought a Parrot Far from Home'

To the East they brought a parrot far from home,
The years passed by, it grew, its beak turned red.
Since the cage was opened every time for feeding,
Knowing it longed for home, they clipped its wings.
Its clever talk endeared, but despite their love
The bird recalled high flights, it took a different view.
How like a singsong girl locked in behind a door,
Tucked away, imprisoned, cosseted in some back room.

Bo Ju-yi

Sentiment

Airing clothes in the courtyard,
I noticed a pair of shoes from my home town.
Who was it gave me these?
A beautiful girl who lived nearby,
And now I remember her words:
'Take these in token of hope
   to start and end together,
To be always like
   this pair of shoes,
Stepping together,
   stopping together.'
Exiled here to Jiang Jun,
Storm-tossed and blown a thousand miles,
to think of my distant love
I brought these shoes all the way.
Nostalgia oppressed me again this morning:
I endlessly handle and gaze at them.
I am still one, the shoes still a pair:
When shall we ever be paired again?
Reason enough for tears and sorrow.
Their brocade design too delicately sewn
To last this blossom-killing rain:
The colour faded, the silk flowers wilted.

Bo Ju-yi

'Buy No Costly Two-Edged Blade'

Buy no costly two-edged blade
  vain expense of so much gold
I have a sorrow in my heart
  that you, I know, cannot cut
Sharpen no unravelling awl
  vain waste of strength and breath
I have a knot in my heartstrings
  that you, I know, cannot loosen
Dye no red silk thread
  vain boast of vivid colour
I have a stream of tear-pearls
  that you, I know, cannot thread
Approach no red alchemic fire
  vain the oppression of its burning vapours
I have whiskers of frost
  such frost you cannot melt

A sword cannot cut the heart's sorrow
An awl cannot unravel the heart's knot
Silk strands cannot thread pearl tears
Flames cannot melt the snow of hair
Far better to drain the sacred cup
A myriad sorrows and memories dispelled in a single draught.

Bo Ju-yi

A Song with Introduction,
to the Horse Cloud-Seeking Dapple

During the De Zong reign-period, when the Emperor was in flight to Sze-Chuan, there were eight horses with him. Seven of them died on the way. Only Cloud-Seeking Dapple travelled on unwearied. During the Zhen Yuan reign-period this horse grew old and died in the Imperial Stables. I, Yuan, wrote this song, that he might be remembered.

Remember how once the Emperor made an imperial progress
    to Sze-Chuan:
Eight horses entered the valleys, seven horses grew tired;
Their flesh broke, their muscles pulled, hooves split.
Seven horses were dead, and the Emperor had no mount:
Son of Heaven fleeing in his imperial cloud of dust.
The sky's rain cried
On his high and dangerous road, soaking the retinue.
Proud loyal regions far beyond sight,
How could they hope to reach the Imperial City?
For hardly had rebel Zhu Zi withdrawn his surrounding armies
When rebel Huai Guang's mounted banditti came hot behind.
The palace ladies gazed around them, leant against the trees,
    wept,
The Retinue Imperial stood silent looking up to Heaven.
And then the grooms brought out Cloud-Seeking Dapple,
Downcast of look, despised by the other horses.
He came forward, snorted and whinnied as if intending a
    meaning,
Pricked his ears, stood alone, with an odd determination.
His Majesty had almost dismissed him when he came nuzzling
    up again,
Ground his teeth, gnashed his jaws, his flanks fine and glossy,
Pawed with his hooves, stood four-square, four-square his head,
His thighs and buttocks strong as mountains,
His tail straight like a stump.

The grooms feared reprimand, and voiced second thoughts to
   each other:
'This horse is no good—useless to try him—
He's for ever biting and pulling, the bridle is hard to place,
He leaps and rears continually, he can't be saddled.'
Disconsolate their expressions, sad their pleas rising to heaven,
But heaven spoke no word, how was His Majesty to know?
Then Dapple submitted, accepted the white jade bridle,
Opened his mouth and took the imperial gold bit.
Then and only then did His Majesty dare to mount him
As if he had met a faithful retainer, long despised, rejected.
A dragon soaring amongst fishes and turtles—and they were
   amazed:
A charger looking down on mules and donkeys—and they lost
   colour.
His Majesty's was a hard predicament,
The road was narrow, the future most uncertain,
For the journey led past Camel Mountain,
Where stones are hatchets placed blade uppermost,
And below the Mount of Qin, where stones are like awls,
Five hundred, maybe six hundred miles through Zhen Fu
   Prefecture,
So past the eighty-four post-stations of the Green Mountain.
Leaping away in a flash like liquid lightning,
Rending suddenly the floating clouds—no telling where the
   Emperor had gone.
The ground became flat, danger over; they brought out the
   imperial yellow chariot,
With it ninety-nine attendant chariots and twelve banners.
Minister Ji Yang went in front leading Dapple by the head,
Minister Yen Zheng welcomed him with a shout and clasped
   Dapple by the feet.
By the wayside stood old men, survivors of the Tien Bao
   rebellion,
Who looked at Dapple, bowed, wept at seeing him.
With one accord they said:
'If the Emperor then had possessed such a horse as this,
He need not have ridden muleback in his flight to Sze-Chuan.'

84

Fierce, brave and impetuous General Li Ling-gong
Took the city, slew the brigands. The evil men were all dead.
Heaven revolves, Earth turns,
The Sun shines again in his capital,
The Son of Heaven is back where he was,
    sitting there in Bright Glory Palace,
The Court is at leisure, forgetting wars and campaigns,
In the morning His Majesty practises hunting,
In the evening takes a turn at feasting,
The Imperial Horses are all well quartered together in the
    Stable of Intentioned Use,
The Emperor himself is at home in the Palace of Manifest
    Excellence.
The grooms again brought forward Cloud-Seeking Dapple,
Sturdy of spirit, massive of stride, quite unsuitable.
They inspected his mane, and it hung loosely,
He held his head too high,
They poked his joints, bent his head, his neck was hard to turn,
They disapproved one by one, he was too difficult to mount.
So the Court banished the stable-men, reduced Dapple's
    hay-ration.
No longer would he wear the silver saddle, the embroidered
    trapping;
Vacantly he would wear away his life-span in some imperial
    stall.
For evil advice was now the order of the day:
'Achievements don't count, let's live it up, enjoy ourselves.'
So away he went, he who climbed mountains, Cloud-Seeking
    Dapple.
There on the flat, readily accepted, stood some fancy steed,
    an imperial favourite.
Now, in the capital, in the third month, the flowers and grasses
    are heavy,
The young horses enjoying the imperial favour prance around,
And many officials enjoy the warmth of office
But General Li Ling-gong is unemployed.
And among the hundred horses fiery and spirited, poor Cloud-
    Seeker grew old.

O Cloud-Seeking Dapple, your like is found but seldom in
   an age.
Once, in another time, your ancestor carried Xiang Yu—
Both man and horse ranked amongst heroes—they called him
   Hegemon of Chu.
Yet today you met His Majesty,
You restored him from exile, brought him safely home.
That's the way it goes, you do a job,
It's completed, on the shelf you go.
Why be like the common run,
On the dusty make till death?
O Cloud-Seeking Dapple—one is used and not used,
But to each his moment:
Don't grieve about it.

Yuan Zhen

You're No Exception

Birds cannot walk, beasts cannot fly
Not understanding each other's understanding, they feel no
    mutual scorn
Dogs do not drink dew, cicadas do not gnaw flesh
Change the cicada with the dog, the cicada'll die, the dog'll
    starve
The swallow sits on the beam, the mouse hides below-stairs
To each his bolt-hole, don't try changing places
Women like needlework, men read the classics
The boy's the ancient, the girl's the wife—each one's knowledge
    is a separation
Fearing your deafness I cup my ear,
Copying your pain I wrinkle my forehead
I am not unless you are, you are without if I am unless

Yuan Zhen

The Song of the Pearl-Fishers

Waves of the sea, fathomless, pearls submerged in the sea.
The pearl-divers pit their lives against death to collect them.
Ten thousand risks to the snatching of one pearl.
Rich men buy concubines by the pearl-load,
Where are the divers?
As year goes by and year comes in, the pearls avoid them.
For the Sea Spirit himself has lately taken up collecting
And when he collects, the pearls die out.
With the bright pearls dead, the sea is empty water.
For the pearls are the sea's, and the sea is the Spirit's.
If the Spirit collects, what chance do mortals have?

Yuan Zhen

'Nearly a Sky Half Clear, Not Yet Half Light'

Nearly a sky half clear, not yet half light,
Drunk I smell the scent of flowers,
   sleeping I hear the oriole,
My Little One trembled to hear the sacred bell.
That was twenty years ago,
   love knowingly dawn-stolen in an old temple.

Yuan Zhen

'Up on the Hillside
He Leans on his Plough'

Up on the hillside he leans on his plough,
His hand full of grain, in his belly a long hunger.

At the window a woman plies her shuttle,
Her hand on the cloth, her body scarcely covered.

In exchange for the Pompadour's beauty
We'd sooner a plain Queen Jane,

Then courtly smiles would come less expensive
And the body politic of course
   put on some weight.

Yu Fen (A.D. 860)

A Warning to Censors

The books were burnt to smoke, the government evaporated
Impregnable frontiers could not save Father Dragon's citadel
The ashes were hardly cold when there was trouble
    in the provinces
The usurpers of course were a couple of illiterates

Zhang Jie

'My Husband's at the Frontier, I'm in the South'

My husband's at the frontier, I'm in the south
Whilst here the west wind blows, I grieve for my man
One line of a letter is a thousand lines of tears
At the front it'll have turned cold, I wonder if you got the
    coat I sent.

Chen Yu-lan

'Walking in Spring,
Apricot Blossom in the Wind'

Walking in spring, apricot blossom in the wind
Any lively young lad will do, coming up the road,
I'll go along with him, let the rest of my life go hang
And suppose he's heartless and throws me over, I'll not be
    ashamed.

Wei Zhuang

'Caligula's Horse'

For a dozen years or so I've been trying to join the Civil Service
But I'm out in the cold, they don't need my sort of talent.
Perhaps I should buy a few chimps and teach them some tricks,
The Court would be amused, they'd clothe me in purple.

Luo Yin

V. The Sung Dynasty
Northern Sung A.D. 960-1126
Southern Sung A.D. 1127-1279

The Sung Dynasty

After the fifty years of disruption known as the Five Dynasties following the collapse of the Tang, Zhao Kuang-yin reunited the nation and named himself first Emperor of the Sung Dynasty.

For three hundred years the dynastic continuum was maintained, and during this period the cultural achievements of China continued to flourish and earn for it the right to be considered the centre of civilization. But in spite of attempts at far-reaching reforms, successive financial and administrative crises undermined the central government. With relative ease the 'Golden Tartars' gained possession of the whole of the Northern area, and in 1126 the capital of Kai Feng fell to the barbarians. From then on Chinese control of the nation was confined to the south, with its capital in Hangchow, the great merchantile hub born from China's 'Commercial Revolution'.

Unfortunately the large landlord interests of Southern China preferred to buy time from the barbarians. The Southern Sung Court favoured a short-sighted appeasement policy towards the Northern aggressors, and consequently paved the way for the disastrous Mongolian occupation of the whole country in 1279.

Amongst other cultural blessings bequeathed to the world by Sung China are some of the finest printed books, exquisite painting, and a rich vein of lyrical poetry. This poetic legacy chiefly takes the form of 'irregular verse' or *ci*. The earliest *ci* were first written during the Tang, but in the Five Dynasties and the Sung this new genre reached its zenith.

Many of the tunes to which the new verse was written are believed to have originated from Central Asia. The fact that *ci* were constructed round a tune freed the poet from the necessity of limiting himself to a regular number of words to the line. He could choose from a large number of existing tunes or even make one up to suit the requirement of his poem. Naturally it followed that he was somewhat freer too in the tonal pattern of his lines. The popular origins of the *ci* and its looser structure account for a far greater injection of colloquial idiom and vocabulary in its language than can be found in most *shi*. Yet it is left to the *ci's* immediate successor, the *San Qu* or popular song of the Yuan Dynasty, to exhibit the full poetic potential of the vernacular.

In spite of the importance of *ci*, a great deal of the best of Sung poetry was still written in the *shi* form. The following section is drawn from both genres.

Lu Nan-gong

Lived in the first half of the eleventh century. He seems to have been on friendly terms with some of the leading literary men of his day but never enjoyed an official career.

Su Dong-po (A.D. 1037–1101)

The compassionate Vice-Governor of Hangchow, Su Dong-po or Su Shi, was a great wit and humanist. It was not only in poetry that he excelled but equally in calligraphy and painting. His concern for the ordinary people, amongst whom he liked to number himself, has made him a popular figure in fiction and drama. Three vernacular short stories from the late Ming period bear witness of the love of later generations for the man Lin Yu-tang has called the 'gay genius'.

Once Su said that for him the composition of a new stanza was as swift and easy as the firing of a crossbow bolt. There is

94

an effortless quality about his verse—the words flow with the same ease as those of Bo Ju-yi, with whom he has so much in common. By his choice of subject he can be said to have rejuvenated the *ci* poem at a time when it was in danger of degenerating into a vehicle for just mere mawkish trivia.

In attitude Su was a Confucian with very marked Taoist and Buddhist leanings. As such he exemplifies the new three-fold outlook of his age.

Bibliography

Lin Yu-tang, *The Gay Genius, the Life and Times of Su Tungpo*, Heinemann, London, 1948.

Su Tung-p'o, *Su Tung-p'o, Selections from a Sung Dynasty Poet*, translated and with an introduction by Burton Watson, Columbia University Press, New York, 1965.

Zhang Shun-min (eleventh century)

A good friend of Su Dong-po. He also took as a poetic model Bo Ju-yi.

Qin Guan (A.D. 1049–1100)

One of Su Dong-po's disciples. For a while he was a professor at the National Academy, but though he held various political appointments he ended his days in exile.

He is particularly noted for his romantic poetry. In spite of his masculine appearance—his thick black beard earned him the nickname 'bearded Chin'—many critics thought his verse effeminate and dubbed it 'maiden's poetry'. Other more sympathetic judges feel that there is a ring of emotional integrity in his lines surpassing those of his great mentor, Su.

Zhang Lei (A.D. 1054–1114)

Another of Su's disciples, he believed 'a good phrase is made in heaven'—and frowned on any attempt at adding literary polish to a poem. Unfortunately a considerable amount of his verse has suffered as a result of his rigid addiction to the 'natural phrase'.

In poems such as the 'Street Vendor's Song' he amply compensates for his shoddier work.

Cai Shen (early twelfth century)

Born in Fukien province, he obtained his Doctorate (*jin-shi*) degree in the reign of the last Northern Sung Emperor, Hui Zong (A.D. 1101–26). Later he was made an Academician of the Imperial Academy.

The poem on p. 106 was originally written in sixteen syllables, a genre known as a *Shi-liu zi ling* (Ditty of sixteen words) a precursor of the Yuan Dynasty popular songs, which share an affinity with the Japanese haiku and tanka poems.

Li Qing-zhao (A.D. 1084–1151)

The talented and devoted wife of the antiquarian Zhang Mingcheng, she was the greatest of China's poetesses. Traditional male jealously and neo-Confucian prejudice towards women probably accounts for the paucity of biographical information available on this remarkable literary lady.

Bibliography

Hu Pin-ching, *Li Ch'ing-chao*, Twayne Publishers, New York, 1966. (A comprehensive study of her life and work with a number of translations.)

Fan Cheng-da (A.D. 1126–1193)

He enjoyed the highest political appointment, that of *Can-zhi zheng-shi* or Premier, and was a prolific writer. The poem represented on p. 108 is unusually lively for this rather staid and orthodox figure.

Xin Qi-ji (A.D. 1140–1207)

Patriot, guerrilla leader and upright official, Xin was all these and a great poet. He took up the vigorous style of Su Dong-po and endowed his poems with a manly and heroic quality fitting the demands of his age, and reflecting his martial career:

'My body wrapped in frost, I slept
Mail-clad, the halberd my pillow.'

Though it is for his patriotic verse that he is most remembered in modern China, much of the appeal of his work rests in the sardonic, self-mocking tone in his more personal poems, born of disillusionment, where he juxtaposed colloquialism with classical reference to convey his particular brand of embittered facetiousness. He was a master of subtle irony, whose highly individualistic style makes him a difficult poet to translate.

Xin Qi-ji grew up in the Tartar-occupied Northern area, in the province of Shantung, a traditional breeding ground for peasant rebellions and hardy soldiers. By his early twenties he had earned a considerable reputation as a guerrilla leader organizing resistance to the alien régime. On one occasion, together with fifty hand-picked followers, he captured a Chinese quisling, Zhang An-guo, from under the noses of the enemy and retreated to the Chinese-controlled Southern area.

The craven attitude of the Southern Sung government towards the Tartar intruders was responsible for the shameful neglect of Xin's outstanding military talents. In spite of his loyal and far-sighted advice the court refused to pursue a policy of rigorous resistance to the Jürched Tartars, but preferred appeasement to active defence, and Xin turned in disgust from politically orientated Confucianism to introspective Taoism and sought relief in alcohol.

It is interesting to note that as a brilliant military strategist he anticipated one of Chairman Mao's more famous dicta, in the following extract from a strategic thesis:

'When he [the enemy] advances, we retreat; when he retreats we shall advance, thus by avoiding unnecessary conflict we will snatch away his heart and wear down his fighting spirit.'

If an example is needed of the Chinese equivalent for the *uomo universale* or 'complete man', I doubt whether there could be a better one than this tough yet erudite warrior-poet.

Liu Ke-zhuang (A.D. 1187–1269)

A major poet of the last years of the Southern Sung who was much influenced by the verse and attitudes of Xin Qi-ji.

Jiang Jie (late thirteenth century)

He gained his Doctorate in 1275, but with the collapse of the Southern Sung after the Mongolian invasion he went into voluntary retirement, and resolutely refused to take office under the invaders.

The Wife of Xu Jun-bao (thirteenth century)

A famous miscellany of the Ming Dynasty the *Chuo-Geng Lu* contains the only available information about the author of this poem, the unfortunate Madam Xu.

'She was captured by the Mongolians and sent to Hangchow, to join the household of Prince Han Qi. On the thousand li journey separating Yue Yang (in Hunan) from Hangchow, her new master repeatedly tried to violate her person, but on every occasion she managed to repel his advances. Now this lady was of such beauty that her lord could not bring himself to slay her, but one day he became so enraged that he was determined to ravage her. Accordingly she begged him saying: "Allow me first to make farewell sacrifice to my former husband, then I shall not hesitate to become your wife. So why anger yourself, My Lord?"

To this proposal he happily concurred. Whereupon she put on her best clothes, burnt incense and made her votive offering, faced the south and wept. Then she wrote a stanza upon the wall to the tune 'The Courtyard full of Fragrance'. Having done this she leapt into the pool in the gardens and died.'

In one sense this poem is more an indictment of the pusillanimity of the Southern Government responsible for the Barbarian Invasion than a lament to the lady's husband.

Butterfly

Butterfly
   time of late spring
      girl slender in a light yellow dress
      leans in the window trying to paint him
As if she's with him in the flowers
      coupled, together and flying
She can't help it if her tears wet the paint
Making his wings heavy to lift

Zhang Bi
(of the Five Dynasties, tenth century)

The Old Wood-Seller

Just an old man from the mountains
   his whiskers bedraggled snow
Shouldering firewood
   he woke early, set out at dawn
The city gate's in sight
   but he has a long way to journey
The fuel's heavy
   his body gaunt, a tired tortoise
Withered skin
   but he has to squeeze out the drops of sweat
Laboured tread
   from a distance you hear the effort of his breath
Other travellers young and sturdy
   keep on passing him
His body's tired
   his mind won't give him time to rest
Young blood in the rich suburbs
   more arrogant than usual
Waves an imperious sleeve from his porch
   gives an impatient shout
The old man lowers his eyes, mentions a sum
   steps back to listen
He's beaten down
   to half his asking price
But he hands the firewood over
   daren't delay a sale
With a sick wife waiting at his gate
   for a bite of breakfast

Lu Nan-gong

Prisoners

In the Xi Ning reign-period (A.D. 1068–1077) during my term as Vice-Governor of this area (Hangchow), on one New Year's eve I was on duty at my office in the County Court. The hall was so full of convicts awaiting a hearing that I was detained well into the evening. It was at this time that I wrote a poem on the wall.

Twenty years have passed since that day, and now that I'm growing old and feeble and happened to be staying in the same area, again I spent the New Year here. The court was quiet and still—the three prisons were all empty. Perhaps my successor's skill in office brought about something which was beyond my powers. Accordingly I wrote this poem to harmonize with the original . . .

New Year's Eve—I should be home by now
Official business keeps me back.
Brush in hand I face them in tears
Pity for these the poor in convict chains:
Small men who schemed for food
They're in the Law's mesh, trapped
    why be ashamed
I too love my mean thin pay,
Stick it out—don't retire.
Who's smart, who's the fool—
We all scheme for food?
Could I let them off—just this once?
But I just sat there dumbly ashamed,
And proved no saintly sage.

Su Dong-po

Bathing the Baby

All fathers hope their sons will turn out clever
With cleverness I've got nowhere all my life
So, little son, I'd have you dense and stupid
No strife, no trouble and you'll become prime minister.

Su Dong-po

Harvest Song

There are sounds of harvesting
Harvest sounds echoing from the North to the Southern hills
The summer sun rises in the North-East
And when it climbs out of the ocean crags the wheat is still
   green
When it rolls to the sky's heart the wheat is already ripe
The crying nightingale gives them no night rest
At dawn the mournful quails in the bamboo presage clouds of
   ink
The wives go on ahead sickles at their waist
The concubines hurry behind with heavy baskets
Up on the slopes they first scythe the fresh stalks
Descending already they clasp sheaves of wheat
Then the farmer's toil turns to joy
Though I daresay their skin is wrinkled,
Their faces leathered by the sun.
The nobles at court enjoy the new harvest already
With sweet wine and flushed features they feast their guests
And when the feast is over and they are surfeited
They might reward their lackeys
Would they believe that nothing yet has passed the peasants'
   lips
For the choicest wheat will go to the revenue men
Soon you'll find the peasants begging for grain in the city
No sooner is the autumn harvest finished than the planting
   must be done
Years of plenty are few, many the baleful seasons
The misery of farmers, what's the remedy?
That's why I pen this harvest hymn
It'll serve just as well for a planting song.

Zhang Shun-min

'Far Night Deep as Water'

Far night deep as water
The wind tightens round the post-house inn shut tight
The dream breaks, a rat shares my lantern
Frost brings the dawn, cold climbs into bed
No sleep, no sleep,
     outside a horse whinnies, people stir.

Qin Guan

To a Courtesan

Arching eyebrows, drunken eyes
   her light glance marvellously
   confused my heart and soul.

Often I remember that time
   the twisting balustrade on the West bank
   her black cloud tresses drifting
   in silken stockings slipping.

She put out her spicy tongue, endlessly tempting
   soft words quietly saying
   'I'll never get used to it.'

Just as our love-making mingled rain and cloud
   the East wind suddenly shook us to pieces.

I'm in a prison now condemned
   by skies that did not care.

Qin Guan

The Street Vendor's Song

The moon sets over the city wall, frost like snow,
From the watch-tower dies the dawn drum sound.
Leaving home with his tray strapped on, crying his wares,
Among the city buildings right and left, no other man's abroad.
'The northwind blows through my clothes, its breath on my
   cakes.
Never mind if my coat is threadbare as long as the cakes keep
   warm.
Be your trade high or low, you've got to keep going,
Keeping afloat's a full-time job.'

Zhang Lei

'Sky'

Sky
   don't let that round toad
      shine on the traveller's sleep
Where's my love?
   In the cassia shadow,
Lady of the moon, you're alone

Cai Shen

'Last Night,
Light Rain and a Violent Wind'

Last night, light rain and a violent wind
    thick sleep but the wine lingers
I ask my chambermaid drawing the bedcurtain
    'How's the begonia blossom?'
    'Still the same,' she says
'Surely you know, there'll be
    too much green too little red.'

Li Qing-zhao

Springtime: Reflections in a Mirror

Old age is a habit hard to admit
    the strong mind prefers to outshadow mountains
Suddenly, counting teeth with the village cronies
    I thought with a start 'How many years . . .'
Having eyes to see I had not seen myself
    till someone said, 'It's the wine gives you that flush'
Today in the mirror I was confronted
    by a withered face—a dried-up lotus leaf
Time drags the frame on through its changes
    but the body just stumbles along behind
Perception and regret now that it's too late
    perception, yes, but then so what?
A fine practical joke by sun and moon
    but I ask you who's going to laugh?
Let's grind away sorrow's sword
    don't wave battle-axes at the sun
If children can compete at birthdays
    with laughter, shouts, dance and song
I'll get excited just as much
    I'll stand up straight, join in, shake a leg.

Fan Cheng-da

I Know You, Don't I, Glass?

('One day going into the mountains with friends and wine, I
couldn't help breaking my vow to stop drinking. I broke my
vow and got drunk and broke into verse again.')

I know you, don't I, glass?
The wine-spring was turned off, the wineskin begged for mercy
Past disciples of drink broke now and then their vows
    —it wasn't easy
And for office, Bacchus is always a poor referee
I know all that but it's small comfort—
    a bunch of grapes, a bag of yeast,
        down go the years and months—
Master, why is your poetry so persuasive
    that I bend my elbow,
        raise the glass.
'O yes,' you say, 'your illness has its reasons
But there's no snake in the glass, don't balk at shadows
Remember Tao Yuan-ming the drunken poet's advice:
    "There's the sum of joy."
Qu Yuan, however, sober, preferred to drown in water.'

Hearing your words, my resolution falters
I'll down this glass—that'll be my lot
What an irony that this night's drinking
    is on the ancients.

Xin Qi-ji

'Round My Bed Scuttles a Hungry Mouse'

Round my bed scuttles a hungry mouse
A bat is trapped turning in the light
Above my roof violent rain blows in the pines
I talk to myself behind the broken panes
I was a man who travelled the country over
Back here I am with grey hair and lined features
To be sure I'm wrapped in tattered bedding,
But when the morning autumn wakes me
I'm still dreaming of my country's lost rivers and mountains.

Xin Qi-ji

'Going Downhill, as Confucius Would Say'

Going downhill, as Confucius would say
It's a shame
  my friends are few
    how many are left today?
What's the use of long white hair streaming down?
  the multifarious world is just a laugh
They ask me What would make you happy, sir?
Well, I've seen dark mountains, they're fine
  and I reckon they and I have something in common
The character and the profile are not dissimilar.
Scratching my head, my glass full,
I stand at the Eastern window
Thinking of Tao Yuan-ming's lingering clouds
  (you know the poem)
It somewhat captures the situation.

There are some schools addicted to fame
  no chance of their seeing clarity in a murky glass.
I turn my head, the clouds start flying, the wind blowing.
I don't regret not having known the ancients
  not knowing my madness is their loss
Those who know me are but two or three,
    Confucius again.

Xin Qi-ji

'Left-Overs'

When drunk just stick to happiness
I ask you, who's for sorrow?
Recently I've had a feeling
   —those good old books
They're not so good, you know.

On the drink again last night
By a pine tree down I tumbled
'I'm really drunk, you know,'
   I tell old pine
Who moves to pick me up
   or so it seemed.
Out came my hands
   'Clear off,' I said.

Xin Qi-ji

Giving It Up, or

Keeping the glass at a distance

You, glass, come here, from now on I'll look after myself
All those years of afterthirst, my throat like an old smoked pot
   sleeping the sleep of the drunk and snoring like thunder
No wonder, old Liu Ling, when you'd had a few you didn't care
     where you were buried
It's quite true, glass, with such friends, no need for enemies
If I go on relying on you to supply me euphoria
I'll agree with the world when they say Wine's slow poison
O it's true there's no large or small hatred doesn't stem from
   you
Not that anything's good or bad in itself but a surfeit brings
   disaster
Look here, I'll make a pact with you 'Stay away, keep off
   I'm strong enough still to smash you, expose you in the
     market place'
To this the glass respectfully replied: 'Curse me and I'll go,
   summon me and I'll be there.'

Xin Qi-ji

'It Could Be at Pine Ridge . . .'

It could be at Pine Ridge sheltering from the heat
   or under thatched eaves out of the rain
There aren't so many ways of killing time
Well now it's 'a peculiar stone' I'm leaning against
   drunk, watching a fountain
And it happens to be just here
   I sobered up last time.
Fellow down the road's taken a wife
   up the street a girl's left home
Giggles and chatter by a lamplit door.
It takes a whole farm to produce my fragrant brew
The day's wind and dew all swallowed every night.

Xin Qi-ji

'Youth Does Not Know How Sorrow Tastes'

Youth does not know how sorrow tastes
But loves 'to haunt autumnal glades
   to haunt autumnal glades'
'And pen new verses'
    forcing out the melancholy

But now I know all right how sorrow tastes
And when about to mention it
  I just say Steady
  Steady that's all I say
Or maybe Nice weather,
    Cool autumn.

Xin Qi-ji

'Pro Patria'

Last night the Imperial Army fought a bloody engagement
First light found the burial-parties busy
They stripped them clean of armour
Then dumped them in the ground
Ranks of burial-cairns, a stone forest on a hill.
In vain their names recorded on the roll of honour
When families go cold, dependents get no pay.
I pity you generals for your day of glory
Yours not to know of all those ghosts whistling in the cold
    wind.

Liu Ke-zhuang

'In the High Wind, Over Fast Sky Waves'

In the high wind, over fast sky waves
   it's ten thousand miles on the toad's back.
I've known that beautiful moon-lady's body
   silk face that needs no make-up.
She wanders through silver corridors of a jewelled palace
   and sees the ether massed in nothingness.
Drunk she shakes suddenly the cassia tree
   that's what people call a cool breeze.

Liu Ke-zhuang

'To Every Petal a Light Butterfly Dress'

To every petal a light butterfly dress
   to every one its scarlet fleck
They say the Creator has no mercy on flowers
   a hundred a thousand different artefacts
In the morning see the trees burst with blossom
   in the evening see how few the petals
They say the Creator really loves flowers
   why then does the rain pour, the wind blow?

Liu Ke-zhuang

'The Rain Song in Youth I Heard from Some Bedroom'

The rain song in youth I heard from some bedroom
   red candle setting behind a satin screen
Older and travelling I heard rain in a boat
   huge river, low clouds,
      a goose crying in the west wind parted from the flock

Now when I hear the rain, in a hermit's cell
   my hair has long turned grey
Sorrow, happiness, parting, joining are all neutral
   raindrops all night long on the stone steps

Jiang Jie

After the Wars

The soldiers have gone, the villagers return
The snows have ceased, the flowers are opening up
Last year's yellowed grass still stands
Smoke puffs again from the little hamlets
Tired rats squeak among the empty walls
Starving crows peck in the barren fields
I seem to hear people muttering:
'The taxman's coming round again'

Xin Yuan (late thirteenth century)

A Lament

A gay life it was and a rich one
    in those lands
  and the Southern gentry
  followed the old primrose paths.
A city of painted windows, red lacquered doorways.
  Ten miles of silver-curtained mansions.
Then one morning the tramp of Mongol soldiery
With banners waving,
    ten thousand leopards,
      relentlessly long penetration
  into those singing halls, dancing pavilions,
Wind rolling up the flower curtains, sorrow petals falling.
Our three-hundred-year dynasty of appeasement
    with its bureaucrats, files, memoranda
      blown clean out of the window.
At least they did not drag me to the North,
  I'm still a guest in my Southern land.
But darling Xu, where is your half of my broken mirror?
  Sorrow's in vain
    and no means now of putting our two reflections together.
From now and for ever
  my broken ghost will travel five hundred miles
    nightly to visit our old Yue-Yang home.

The wife of Xu Jun-bao

120

VI. Yuan Dynasty: The Mongolian Occupation of China A.D. 1280-1367

The Age of Drama and Popular Songs

All but the last of the poems in the following section belong to the *San Qu* genre or 'popular song', a lyric freer in form and language than any of the preceeding classical styles of verse, with its antecedents in the *ci*—for like the *ci, San Qu* poems were written to a specific tune. Though, as we have already seen, the *yue-fu* 'Han folk song' and the *ci* 'Sung Irregular poem' are two major forms of literary expression with demotic origins adopted and adapted by the *literati*, the emergence of the *San Qu* in the Yuan Dynasty represents a major breakthrough in the history of Chinese literature, for unlike their poetic predecessors these 'songs' are closely linked with a major trend towards the popularization of literature which started in the Yuan and continued throughout the Ming and part of the Ch'ing. This process of popularization not only affected poetry but lead to the emergence of drama and vernacular fiction as major vehicles of literary expression. The reasons underlying this development have their origins in the cataclysmic experience that Chinese society underwent during the Mongolian occupation.

Under the Mongolian domination the educated Chinese found themselves for the first time in the history of their country no longer looked upon as the ruling élite but relegated to the lower echelons of the social ladder. At the most they might be lucky enough to fill minor official posts when they would be constantly supervised and spied upon by their suspicious Mongolian overseers. Indeed for many years throughout the occupation the Civil Service examinations were suspended by the uncouth conquerors, so that the cream of the nation's intelligentsia became more or less social pariahs. 'We [the Confucian *literati*] are one stage above beggars and mendiants, one stage below whores and singing girls', wrote one Chinese intellectual during the Yuan.

Cut off as they were from finding a career in the traditional occupation of governmental service many literary men turned their talents to the writing of plays and *San Qu* in the despised vernacular language. No longer were they writing for their own relatively narrow coterie but for the merchants and artisans, porters and pedlers of the flourishing urban centres of China, which Marco Polo gazed upon with such wonderment. To a large extent their subjects remained the same as those of the *ci* and *shi* of their predecessors, who had lived in the more privileged times, but it is hardly surprising that we find amongst the *San Qu* many themes that prove the existence of common ground between the intellectual poet and the illiterate masses (e.g., Sui Jing-chen's 'Imperial Progress'). Alien régimes in occupation have a way of ironing out at least some of the disparities between class and caste. Nor is it the thematic empathy between the poet and his common reader, the freer metrical structure and colloquial phraseology of the poem itself alone that give the *San Qu* its characteristically popular quality. In the following lines from a poem whose theme is decidedly traditional, reflecting as it does the Taoist intellectual's realization of the ephemeral nature of life, the '*lachrimae rerum*' and the vanity of worldly attainment, Ma Zhi-yuan, one of the greatest dramatists and *San Qu* poets writes:

Before me the sun westward runs
   as swiftly as a cart downhill

When morning comes the mirror clearly shows
   more snows have fallen

Into bed I climb and bid farewell
   to shoes and socks.

Even if we have already met the image of the mirror reflecting the sad snow of white hair in many a past traditional poem, we would be unlikely to have encountered such a homely image as that of the last two lines. The possession of expensive bronze mirrors in China was limited to the wealthy leisured classes who had time enough to lament time's passing. Whereas the custom of old men to say goodbye each night to their footwear in the hope of finding the sweet solace of death in sleep was a practice exclusively confined to the work-worn peasantry. Thus an affinity of the human condition is conveyed by the antithesis of rich and poor, Taoist 'recluse' and peasant toiler.

Despite the fact that perhaps the greatest literary achievements during the Yuan and the following ages were written in the heterodox vernacular language, little is known about the individual lives of the great dramatists, *San Qu* writers, and novelists of the Yuan and Ming, for almost simultaneously with the emergence of the champions of vernacular writing came the ugly phenomena of censorship and literary inquisitions, and anonymity remained an essential prerequisite for most of these great pioneers.

Bo Pu (A.D. 1226–?)

Dramatist as well as a poet, Bo Pu, who is sometimes referred to as Bai Pu, refused to collaborate with the Mongols. His verses are noted for their refinement, polish and bawdiness.

Guan Yun-shi (A.D. 1286–1324)

This remarkable poet was originally a Turkic speaking Uighur. His father's name was Gonchak (?), the first syllable of which explains why he assumed the traditional Chinese monosyllabic surname of Guan. So proficient was his knowledge of the Chinese language that he ranks as one of the few foreigners ever to have enriched the literature of his adopted nation. When writing of another great dramatist and poet he described the quality of his verse as 'a cup of wine in a maiden's hand'. This comment is equally valid of his own writing.

In addition to his second name he took the *hao*, cognomen or nickname, of Suan-zhai, Sour Studio. Another lesser writer of *San Qu* from the same period, Xu Zai-si, was known by his cognomen of Tian-zhai, Sweet Studio. This unfortunate coincidence gave rise to the practice of publishing their combined literary efforts in one volume with the bizarre title of *Suantian yue-fu*—'Ballads by Sweet and Sour'.

Sui Jing-chen (late thirteenth, early fourteenth century)

A Yuan Dynasty miscellany on dramatists and poets by Zhong Si-cheng, *Lu Gui Bu* (*The Register of Recorded Ghosts*) tells us that, 'In the seventh year of the Da De Reign Period, Master Sui came from Wei Yang to the city of Hangchow where we both became acquainted.' From this scant record of one of the great literary 'ghosts' we can ascertain that Sui was active between the end of the thirteenth and the beginning of the fourteenth centuries.

Sui is chiefly remembered for his contribution to narrative *San Qu*. In his hands the short *Ling* or ditties were linked together to form a *tao* or 'chain' with a unity of theme, often with a satirical intention, as in his famous 'Imperial Progress'. Like earlier satirical ballads by Bo Ju-yi and Yuan Zhen, though the statement of the poem deals with a specific historical event, the implication is universal and not confined to a particular historical event.

Zhong Si-cheng (late fourteenth century)

A native of Hangchow, the thriving commercial centre of Yuan China. His poetry is noted for its humorous turn of phrase. When Zhung Si-cheng wrote his famous *Lu Gui Bu* (*The Register of Recorded Ghosts*) his intention was to keep alive at least the names of the great poets and dramatists of his life-time; in so doing, alas, his unselfish dedication got the better of him for he fails to tell us anything about his own life and activities. A later writer says 'he shut up his door and preferred to cultivate his lofty enterprise in private'—presumably this refers to the compilation of his miscellany.

'After a Long Drink,
No Barriers Are Left Standing'

After a long drink, no barriers are left standing
If you don't sober up, what worries can you have?
Lees and pickles, they're two titles to fame
Hard liquor irons out the ups and downs of all the ages
Yeast buries the 10,000 foot ambition of a coloured rainbow
The unsuccessful can laugh at sober Qu Yuan's folly
But those who know what's what all confirm drunk Tao was
    right

Bo Pu

Unruly Sun

Nestling, leaning by the cloud window both we sit
Looking, smiling on the moon pillow in tune we sing
Listening, counting, fearing, sorrowing, early comes the dawn
    drum
The fourth stroke's past, our passion's not yet quenched
Our passion's not yet quenched, night like a shuttle
O sky, just one more leap-hour, where's the harm?

Guan Yun-shi

The Imperial Progress

(The exalted ancestor, first Emperor of the Han,
pays a visit to his native village)

The village headman bursts in door after door to make his
    announcement
When there's official business you can't put it off
And this is no ordinary job
There's fodder to be found for the retinue's horses
Porters to be supplied as well
There's talk of a procession of horse and carriage
Everybody knows it's an Imperial progress
Today He's coming back home
Old villager Wang mends his roof as good as new
Young Busy Zhou heaves a calabash of wine
They're wearing newly dyed turbans
And freshly starched shirts
Dressed up just like the big nobs

Blind Wang Lui musters a motley crew of charmers
Fumble-fisted Hu plays the pipes, bangs the drum
As men and horses come into view at the village gate
Ahead of them flags are fluttering
One flag's white and round, it looks like the man in the moon
One's round and red like the rising sun
One's a phoenix—it looks like a chicken trying to dance
One's a flying dragon—more like a dog with wings
One's the imperial dragon clutching a pearl—more like a snake
    coiled round a wine-gourd

There are men with scarlet tridents, silver-inlaid halberds
A golden mace shaped like a cucumber
Someone flashes a mighty spear, another waves a snow-white
    goosefeather fan

What a magnificent band of personages
Grasping all sorts of odd cutlery,
Decked out in the most outlandish garb
Those are real horses between the shafts
No sign of mules in front
Yellow silk umbrella with a strangely twisted handle
In front of the carriage eight fairy officials
Behind, a number of flunkeys
Then several dainty ladies
Dressed and made-up all alike

The big fellow gets out of his carriage
The crowd salute him several times
The big fellow looks right past them
The old men of the village bow and scrape
The big fellow gives them a hand up
Suddenly as I take a look
I look and look again—I know him all right
Indignation bursts my chest:

'Your real name's Liu
Your missus was called Lu
I can tell your family histories backwards
You used to be the village constable
And fond of more than a jar or two
Your father-in-law taught in the village school
He'd read a couple of books
Your place was just to the east of my farm
You used to feed my buffalo, mow my grass
Put hand to plough, do a spot of hoeing

In the springtime you helped yourself to my mulberry-leaves
In the winter you came borrowing my grain
What I advanced you in rice and wheat I couldn't begin to say
You fiddled the land-deeds, gave short measure
Stole more than a bushel to pay back wine-debts
You got up to a thing or two
But I've still got your I.O.U.'s
It's down in the records, you know,

The cash you never returned
The lads who bribed you to get off the draft
Not to mention the grain you owe us
And the revenue you've pocketed on the sly
But to us you're just old Liu's third son
Anyone could put the finger on you
So why go calling yourself First Emperor of the Han?'

Sui Jing-chen

Scholar Gipsy

Of spirited gentry, the poor are the best
The provincial rich are a difficult lot.
With scraps of brick and mortar I'll patch me an old kiln
                        —a hot-bed hovel
Or run a municipal school for beggars
Don a threadbare black scholar's cap
Put on a loose fit of an old sack inside out
Bind round me an elegant outsize sash
I'll be unsalaried—a moonlight academician.

Zhong Si-cheng

VII. The Ming Dynasty
A.D. 1368-1644

The Ming Dynasty

With the expulsion of the Mongols Chinese society reverted to the established norm of former dynasties. Yet though the *literati* once again assumed their exalted position as the ruling élite, the writing of *San Qu* and plays continued to flourish throughout the Ming. In addition the realm of vernacular fiction was enriched by the emergence of many beautiful novels and short stories, which found a ready market in the great urban centres of the South and the lower reaches of the Yang-tze River. It is not surprising that Feng Meng-long, the compiler and editor of the *Shan Ge* (Folk Songs) selected in this anthology, combined his activity of novelist and dramatist with those of folklorist and literary critic.

The last eighty years of the Ming, a period contemporaneous with our own dynamic Elizabethan and Jacobean eras, make up the golden age of dissenting literary enterprise. Throughout these years some of the most original writers and intellectuals show the first serious attempts to break out of the strait-jacket of the classical language and fashion the vernacular as an accepted means of literary expression. In their love of popular art forms—drama, folk-song and fiction, we can see reflected an undercurrent of definite, if at times somewhat incoherent dissatisfaction with the established values of restrictive Confucian society. Significant too is the fact that this literary movement grew up at a time when equally radical voices were clamouring for political reforms to revitalize the governmental system.

Unfortunately the Chinese body politic was beyond redemption, and the Central Government, plagued by corruption and cliques, had no inclination to learn from the more visionary thinkers of the age. Following the disastrous peasant rebellion of Li Zi-cheng in 1644, the sinicized Manchus pacified and conquered the nation with the shamefully active collaboration of the Chinese conservative hierarchy.

It is a strange paradox that the alien Manchu or Ching Dynasty (1644–1911) is marked by an excessive degree of Confucian orthodoxy. Unlike the Mongols, the Manchu conquerors proved themselves more Chinese than the Chinese in their addiction to established classical dogma. Under such repressive conditions the vernacular had no chance to usurp the privileged position of the literary language, indeed much of the existing unorthodox branches of literature with their erotic and controversial content were to become the victims of some of the most savage literary inquisitions in the eighteenth century.

In spite of the temper of the times, a number of outstanding works of isolated genius in both forms of the written language appeared in the Ching dynasty, but these, primarily fiction and belles lettres, fall outside the confines of this book, and the reader will have to excuse the absence of any poetry from the last of the Imperial dynasties in our volume.

Tang Yin (A.D.1470–1523)

Though Tang wrote a number of lively colloquial poems, he is remembered most for his paintings and his rather scandalously bohemian activities. Feng Meng-long (see below) includes a delightful short story in his *San Yen* collection about this charming artist and poet. For many years literary historians deemed him to be the author of a highly pornographic novel *Seng-ni nie-hai* (*The Evil Doings of Monks and Nuns*).

Feng Meng-long (A.D. 1590–c.1646)

The greatest folklorist and short-story writer of the Ming, he was one of the most original and daring *literati* of his age, who wrote under the pseudonym of 'Mo Han Zhai'—the Ink-crazed Studio. His contribution to fiction and poetry is unrivalled. In the early 1620s Feng compiled and edited a three-volume collection of short stories—*San Yen*. Most of these tales had their origins in the prompt books of the professional story-tellers' guilds, and had been transmitted for hundreds of years in the market places of the great cities. Without his vision and original literary outlook no doubt many of these stories would never have survived. Not content with collecting and polishing oral fiction, Feng tried his hand at writing plays and original novels.

His devotion to folk poetry is equally important. In the first decade of the seventeenth century he appears to have started the compilation of his *Shan Ge* (Hill Songs)[1]—the compendium of earthy folk songs from Jiang-su and Zhe-jiang provinces, some of which we have collected in this volume. These songs he recorded with faultless accuracy without expunging any of their lively vulgarity, though he often could not forego the opportunity of adding witty and facetious marginalia of his own. In his introduction to these poems, in itself a unique piece of controversial literary criticism, he is at pains to point out that popular poetry reflects more originality of sentiment than the sterile banalities of contemporary classical verse.

'Insincerity,' he writes, 'may well exist in conventional literature, but rarely in folk poetry. . . for these poems find their inspiration in the genuine emotions of man and woman and expose the quack remedies of established moral teaching.'

In spite of his unconventional theories and his heterodox writings, Feng Meng-long remained a loyal official of the Ming and preferred death to collaboration with the Manchu invaders.

Amongst the poems inspired by erotic associations seen in household objects such as 'Sword', 'Comb', etc., there is the same salacious flavour as that of the following Anglo-Saxon Riddle, as I have freely rendered it into English:

A wonderful fellow am I, a joy to women
Upstanding, high in the bed
Rough, hairy underneath. At times
A fine peasant girl ventures to me,

[1] *Shan Ge*, 'Hill Song' or 'Folk Song'. A term first used in Bo Ju-yi's famous poem 'Pi Pa Xing' ('The Ballad of the Lute').

A proud minded maid, who grips me
Seizes me red, and rapes my head
Holding me fast; soon to discover
My true meaning—thus approaches
That curly locked girl, with eye so moist.

Where the answer, of course, is an onion. The bawdy side of
the Chinese temperament has a lot more in common with our
own tradition than we might at first expect. Chinese poetry is
by no means just the demesne of Taoistic eremitical and
Confucian didactic expression.

Ling Meng-chu (A.D. 1580–1644)

He was possibly the greatest short-story writer in the vernacu-
lar tradition at the end of the Ming Dynasty. His achievement,
manifested in the famous collection of eighty short stories
called the *Pai-An Jing-qi* (*Amazing Tales Inspiring Applause*),
earns him the reputation of the most inventive raconteur of his
age. Unlike his contemporary, Feng Meng-long, who contented
himself with editing existing popular stories, Ling Meng-chu's
works are the product of his own genius.

Both as a magistrate and a writer, he seems to have had
something of Henry Fielding's tolerance of the shortcomings
and frailties of his fellow human beings. According to one
local gazetteer, he once ventured quite alone and unarmed
into a brigands' lair, where he talked fifty or more fierce
desperadoes into changing their ways; no doubt his ready wit
and the respect for a good rogue evinced in his poem 'The
Master Burglar of Soochow', helped him in the success of this
hazardous mission. For some years, he was responsible for the
coastal defences against Japanese pirates in the present-day
Shanghai area. It was during the defence of his own town of
Wucheng that he died a valiant death fighting against the
armies of the usurper Li Zi-cheng. His last words to the
insurgents were: 'Spare the people'.

The poems included here belong with the exception of
'A Cautionary Verse' to the *San Qu* and *ci* tradition They were
selected from my translation of some of his short stories

published under the title of *The Lecherous Academician*, (London, Rapp and Whiting, 1972). Though designed originally as mere poetic saffron to complement a lively narrative, such verse has a charm and vigour all of its own.

The Revenue Men

Trumpet-blowers, bugle-puffers,
Your range is narrow, your belly-bags are big
Your tax-boats thread the rivers like tangled weeds
Just blast out your price is all you've got to do
When the militia hear it, the ranks are saddened
When the peasants hear it, their hearts turn white
Fair play is no concern of yours
In the wink of an eye you blow this family down
Blast a hole in that household
You'll blow till the water's dry and your goose has flown

Wang Pan

Inscription for a Portrait

Last night the cherry-apple
  deflowered by the first rain-drops
Its fallen petals slight and frail
  their beauty almost articulate.
My mistress rising early
  leaves her bedroom
In her hand a mirror
  to admire her painted cheeks.
She asks me 'which is prettier
  the petals or my complexion?'
To her question I reply
  'They win by innocence.'
At hearing this my mistress
  displays a charming anger
Refusing to believe dead petals
  surpass a real live person.
She crumbles a handful of blossom
  to throw in my face—
'Tonight, my dear' she says
  'sleep with the flowers!'

Tang Yin

Song for a Peach Blossom Pavilion

Here at peach blossom haven
   I've a peach blossom pavilion
In the peach blossom pavilion
   hides a peach blossom girl
I plant peaches
   for my peach blossom girl
Pluck her peach blossom
   change it for wine
When I sober up
   I sit with my blossom
After a glass or two
   I sleep with my blossom
Half drunk half sober
   day after day goes by
Blossom falls and blossom buds
   year after year
Just let's get old and die
   with blossom and wine
What need to bow
   for carriage and horse
Carriage dust and horses' hooves
   are the rich man's interest
A jar of wine and a sprig of blossom
   is the poor man's luck
Comparing rank and pelf
   with simple poverty
The first lies flat on the ground
   the last rides high in the sky
Comparing poor simplicity
   with carriage and horse
To them the hurry and bustle
   for me the leisure and time
Others may think
   I'm a fond old man

I just smile
   that they don't get the point
Don't you see the graves
   of history's great men
Without blossom and wine
   they're only good for the earth

Tang Yin

Folksong

Old skymaster
You're getting on, your ears are deaf
    your eyes are gone
Can't see people Can't hear words
Glory for those who kill and burn
   for those who fast and read the scriptures
    Starvation
Fall down, old master sky
  how can you be so high
How can you be so high,
    come down to earth.

The Master of Mint Studio,
A.D. Sixteenth century

Shan Ge Folk Songs

Swing

Lass sits swinging to and fro
Lad lies pulling the silken strings
She lifts her legs high in the air
Waiting for the boy's two hands to send her near and far
Strings
pluck her soul sky-soaring

Feng Meng-long

Calabash

Enchanting is the fresh calabash
You can't take your eyes off it day after day
When coming together don't learn from an old one
For it comes apart
One half goes east, one goes west

Feng Meng-long

Comb

Unbearable slipping of comb through hair
Keen-edged teeth exquisitely skilled
Knows many ways of making me tingle
But don't pass it through others'
Or its teeth will dull and serve no purpose

Feng Meng-long

Pagoda

Tapering pagoda seven storeys tall
Takes months and years to build complete
Let us be master-builders in our love-making
A misplaced brick tumbles the tower
Love isn't built in one night

Feng Meng-long

Sword

Charmed blade wielded so deftly
Three-foot Excalibur flashing brightly
Sweetheart, don't say you have no loving sword
Sweet blade, don't say you have two edges
Come, my love, pierce me at close quarters

Feng Meng-long

Smiles and Laughter

South-East wind comes blowing aslant
Opening up many a fresh young flower
So nice young lady from a good home don't go giggling around
How many love-affairs start with a laugh

Feng Meng-long

Giving the Eye

Thinking of having a bit of fun with you
We don't need banns we don't need a dowry
Catching your eye means catching your fish in my little net
Three hundred yards of fine white silk will flow from your
    shuttle

Feng Meng-long

Frustration

Young girl in bed who cannot sleep
Soft skin, white body, cold as ice
Tormented like a prisoner in the cell
Or silver spoiling, left too long on the boil

Feng Meng-long

No Boyfriend

I

The west wind saddens my heart
Eating loneliness on a cold night without my darling
Or should I run to and fro for free young lads who'll help me
   out
Rather I'd have him back to keep me from the cold

II

The door opens on swirling snow
Cold winter night should bring him here
Brocade coverlets three layers thick are too thin for the cold
All I want is my darling hot on my belly

Feng Meng-long

Looking

He's no shy young man
Why does he keep looking at my front door
My old man keeps two sharp eyes on the front but never behind
If you want a closer look at me why not go round the back

Feng Meng-long

Boat

Boy holding the rudder
Girl gripping the pole
I'll rock, love, when you pole
She says, and if you pole
Against the stream then to it with a will
And if you bring her head round
I'll turn astern

Feng Meng-long

Love-Affairs

I

When twenty's gone comes twenty-one
No sense in doing without the loving
For flowers past thirty are apt to fade
And though she beckons with both hands, no lad'll come.

II

Sow your oats, you wild and strong
Or reap regret when you are old
Unless you take your pleasures with the willing flesh
From the jewelled mount you'll come back empty-handed.

Feng Meng-long

Looking

Girl by the window embroiders mating birds
Easy-going gallant poles his punt from the bank
Girl looks at boy, the needles prick her hand
Boy looks at sweet young girl, the boat capsizes

Feng Meng-long

No Preliminaries

The mountain noted for mighty tigers is not always high
The speed of the first-class racing boat does not depend on the
　　oar
The champion does not throw his weight about
Nor does the man-eating lady need to flirt

Feng Meng-long

Games

I

Rain-bright blouse of green, red sash round her waist
She stands on the gang-plank, arch as a bridge to fun
Her hair combed smooth as water
Take a careful look and this little morsel will melt in your
    mouth

II

It's great fun
It's great fun
Snug in my corner getting a visit twice a day
I'm a well-fed abbot, in luck with the offerings
Any young boatman can punt me clear upstream

Feng Meng-long

Between the Sheets

One was languid and newly aroused,
The other was fire and bursting with passion.
She was parched firewood to his heat,
Drenched in his lightning, a firestorm kindled in her body.
For the neighbours' ears they cared not a jot,
Happily secure behind locked doors.
What need for go-betweens and ceremony
Now flesh to flesh was joined?
Like water to a thirsty traveller, their release;
Their love-game ended, a dead soul was reborn.

Ling Meng-chu

Bed Time

My lovely mistress came quite unexpected
At midnight to be fondled in my bed.
Behind the curtains, clasped between her thighs,
Beneath, below my roving fingers thread
Under her petticoat, within her slip,
Sweet the sensation of our limbs enlaced,
For she's on fire with love and I'm not chaste.

And when I'd stop, she cries
    her passion's not yet spent;
O like a dream she came
    and in a dream she went.

Ling Meng-chu

A Cautionary Verse

O sweet sixteen her body soft as curd,
Sharp secateurs concealed between her thighs.
He's pruned and lopped without his knowing it,
Within the bone his marrow drains and dries.

Ling Meng-chu

Justice of the Peace

Fine chests all covered in brocade
And shelves of priceless curios,
No common pots, but silverware,
And golden ingots stacked in rows.

From the mighty tusker's mouth he stole
The ivory once proudly worn—
That maids now use to poke the fire.
The massive rhino's princely horn
Is used by boys to ladle soup.
False accusations, poor men's groans
In court and yamen won him wealth:
It's built on innocent blood and bones.

By bribery and jobbery
He brought the dirty money in
That gave him these rich clothes and furs:
They're sewn from peasant flesh and skin.

He does his best for his own sons
High rank and station to ensure,
But wears a pious humble air
As so-called father of the poor.

Ling Meng-chu

Lazy Dragon,
the Master Burglar of Soochow

So limber that he seems to have no bones,
His footsteps pass more silent than a sigh,
He strides across the roof beams like a giant
Or walks up walls, as tiny as a fly.

All situations he can play by ear,
Or if need be, can force his supple lips
To mimic cat or dog or rat; and all
Deceptive sounds are at his fingertips.

His mimicry is truer than the truth;
Just like a ghost he flits, now there, now here,
Quick as a gust of wind, a shower of rain;
In all the underworld he has no peer.

Ling Meng-chu

Bibliography

(Principal Chinese Works Consulted)

Abbreviations: S.B.B.Y. . . . . . Si-bu Bei-yao
G.X.J.B.C.S. . . . Guo-xue Ji-ben Cong-shu

Title	Author	Published Location
Bo Ju-yi Juan	Chen You-qin	Peking, 1962
Bo-xiang Ci-pu Jian	Shu Ming-lan and Xie Chao-zheng	Hong Kong, 1959
Cha-tu-ben Zhong-guo wen-xue shi	Zheng Zhen-duo	Peking, 1958
Gu-dai Shi-ge xuan	Wang Yi-peng	Shanghai, 1962
Gu Shi Yuan	Shen De-qian	Hong Kong, 1966
Han Wei Liu Chao Bai-san-jia ji	Zhang Pu (ed.)	Taipei, 1963 (Ming photolitho edition)
Li Bo Shi-xuan	Shu Wu	Peking, 1954
Li Dai Min-ge Yi-bai Shou	Shang Li-qun	Shanghai, 1961
Liu Chao Yue-fu Yu Min-ge	Wang Yin-xi	Peking, 1961
Mao Shi Zheng-yi	Mao Heng (annotated by Kong Ying-da)	S.B.B.Y. Taipei, 1965
Mao Shi Zhu-su	—	G.X.J.B.C.S.
Quan Song Ci	—	Peking, 1965
Quan Tang Shi	—	Peking, 1965
Quan San-qu	Sui Shu-sen (ed.)	Peking, 1964
San-qu Cong-kan	Ren Zhang-min	Taipei, 1964
Shan-ge	Feng Meng-long (ed.)	Ming Quing Min-ge Shi-diao Cong-shu, Peking, 1962
Shi Jing Xuan	Yu Guan-ying	Peking, 1956
Song Ci Xuan	Hu Yun-yi	Peking, 1962
Su Dong-po Shi-ci xuan-zhu	—	Hong Kong, 1960
Tang Wu Dai Ci Xuan	Cheng Zhao-lin	G.X.J.B.C.S.

Title	Author	Published Location
Wei Jin Nan-bei Chao Wen-xue-shi Can-kao Zi-liao	—	Peking, 1962
Wen Xuan	Xiao Tong (ed.) Li Shan (comment)	Hong Kong, 1962
Yuan Ba Shi-xuan	Su Zhong-xiang	Shanghai, 1957
Yuan Ming San-qu	Gu Fu-ying	Shanghai, 1955
Yue-Fu Shi-Ji	Guo Mao-qian	Si-Bu Cong-kan (edition)
Yue-Fu Shi-xuan	Yu Guan-ying	Peking, 1954
Zhong-guo Li-dai Ci-xuan	Luo Qi	Hong Kong, 1964
Zhong-guo Li-dai Shi-xuan	Ding Ying	Hong Kong, 1962
Zhong-guo Su-wen-xue Shi	Zheng Zhen-duo	Peking, 1962
Zhong-guo Wen-xue-fa-zhan Shi	Liu Da-jie	Peking, 1962
Zhong-guo Wen-xue Pi-ping Shi	Guo Shao-yu	Peking, 1961
Zhong-guo Wen-xue Shi	Academia Sinica of Literary History Dept.	Peking, 1962

Appendix:
Some Notes on Chinese Prosody

Traditional studies of Chinese poetry frequently divide verse into two basic metrical categories—poems with lines made up of a regular number of ideographs each representing a monosyllabic word or particle, and those with an irregular number to the line. In itself this categorization holds good as a rough guideline for the major forms of traditional verse, though within both groups there exist a large number of subdivisions often of considerable divergence.

The first category includes the oldest collection of Chinese verse, the *Shi Jing* or *Book of Odes*, where the majority of poems are of four words to a line, though others ranging from as few as two to as many as nine words to a line can also be found. Indeed the poems of a regular number of words to a line, referred to as *shi*, may be considered the typical mode of traditional poetic expression. It is certainly the oldest form, and reflects an early realization of the characteristic monosyllabic nature of the Chinese language. For within this form those most common devices of antiphonic balance, parallelism and antithesis beloved by Chinese poets could be used to the utmost effect. Even amongst the earliest archaeological evidence of the Chinese written script—the ancient writings preserved on oracle bone and scapulae of the Shang Dynasty (1766–1154 B.C.)—we find divinations and votive inscriptions written in a form of balanced phrasing with an attempt at final rhyming or repetitive refrain:

Gui mao bu, jin ri yu.
On Gui Mao day, for rain we pray.
Qi zi xi lai yu
Will from west come rain?
Qi zi dong lai yu

Will from east come rain?
Qi zi bei lai yu
Will from north come rain?
Qi zi nan lai yu
Will from south come rain?[1]

Such a functional piece of necromancy, of nugatory poetic inspiration, itself may prove nothing more than that even the priest scribes at the dawn of Chinese civilization were aware of the rhythmic power of a five-word line in their incantations. But over the following centuries, when we examine the verse of the *Book of Odes*, we find definite evidence of a more polished attempt at those devices later to be employed by exponents of *shi* or regular verse:

Xi wo wang yi
Formerly (when) (I) went
Yang liu yi-yi
Willow (and) poplar (were) graceful (and) slender
Jin ri lai si
Now (when) (I) come back
Yu xue fei-fei
Rain (and) snow (falls) swirling (and) twirling.

By the second century A.D. *shi* of five and seven words to a line had more or less ousted the four word to a line verse, thus setting the fashion for the major poetic patterns of the golden age of *shi* verse, the Tang Dynasty (A.D. 618–907) when many poems were written in the 'New Verse Style', or *xin ti shi* with its strict rules of tonal contrast, as well as *dui-ou* parallelism and antithesis both in grammatical and sense pattern.

One such New Style *shi* was the *lü-shi* or cadenced verse, or eight lines of either five or seven words in each. In our selection we have included a five-word *lü-shi* of Wang Wei which epitomizes the metrical demands of the New Verse Style. First comes our final version, which still retains some of the more obvious aspects of the original pattern, except for rhyme:

[1] See *Bu Ci Tong Zuan*, compiled by Guo Mo-ruo.

Viewing the Hunt

Muscle of wind, the horned bow twangs,
The commander is hunting by Wei River City.
The grass is wilted, sharp darts the falcon's eye,
The snows have melted, light run the horses' hoofs.

They are suddenly past Xin Feng,
Homeward to Xi Liu Garrison.
Glance back to where the shot kite falls:
A thousand level miles of evening cloud.

 L   O   O   L   L
Feng jing jiao gong ming   (Rhyme)
Wind powerful horn bow sing
 O   L   L   O   L
Jiang jun lie wei cheng   (Rhyme)
Command army hunt(s) Wei city
 O   L   L   O   O
Cao ku ying yen ji
Grass wither falcon eye swift
 L   O   O L L
Xue jin ma ti qing   (Rhyme)
Snow exhaust horse hoof light.

 O   O   L   L O
Hu guo xin Feng shi
Suddenly pass xin Feng town
 L   L   O   O   L
Huan gui Xi Liu ying   (Rhyme)
Still return West Willow camp
 L   L   O   L   O
Hui kan she diao chu
Turn look shoot kite place
 L   O   O   L   L
Qian li mu yun ping   (Rhyme)
Thousand mile evening cloud level.

The letters O and L refer to the two major tonal categories,
the oblique and level tones of the ancient language—which
are no longer operative in modern standard Chinese.

159

In such New Style cadenced verse of eight lines, grammatical parallelism and antithesis were expected in the second and third couplets. Grammatically the pattern Wang Wei has chosen can be represented as follows in the second couplet:

Cao ku ying yen ji
Noun verb noun noun stative-verb
Xue jin ma ti qing
Noun verb noun noun stative-verb

It is obvious that such careful marriage and pairing of words helps the reader determine the syntactic relationship between each word. For instance, at first glance the reader might be baffled by the relationship between the two juxtaposed nouns *ying*—falcon, and *yen*—eye, until he glances at the complementary line with its *ma*—horse, and *ti*—hoof. Note too the vague but nonetheless intentional antithesis and parallelism of meaning of grass/snow, wither/vanish, falcon/horse, eye/hoof, swift/light.

Now let us consider the prosody with regard to tonal pattern and rhyme scheme, bearing in mind that the pronunciation and tonal values of the modern phonetic transcription are very different from the pronunciation current in China twelve hundred years ago. In order to avoid explaining the intricacies of the ancient tonal structure of Chinese, we may for the sake of argument look upon the distinction between oblique and level tones as being somewhat similar to our own Western use of quantity or stress to convey metrical rhythm. Though this poem has a rhyme at the end of the first line (ming/cheng), the more standard pattern for a five-word *lü-shi* was a rhyme at the end of the second, fourth, sixth and eighth lines. As there has been presumably little change in the pronunciation of syllables ending a in a vowel plus *ng*, the rhyme here has been preserved and is immediately apparent even to a Western reader. In considering the tonal pattern, we should remember that the all-important words in a line were the second, fourth and final (sixth as well in a seven-word New Style poem). On these, the second, fourth, (sixth), and final words, the tones should be so arranged as to produce contrast between the first and second lines of a couplet; whilst the last line of a couplet should be identical on these key words with the first line of the next (except for the final word). Consider the second stanza's metrical pattern:

    O   O   L   L   O
Hu guo Xin Feng shi
   L   L   O   O   L
Huan gui Xi Liu ying (R)
   L   L   O   L   O
Hui kan she diao chu
   L   O   O   L   L
Qian li mu yun ping (R).

Wang Wei has followed the rules except in the fourth word of the first line of the last couplet—*diao* should be oblique tone, not level. This is the only metrical irregularity he allows himself. Apart from this, the other five irregularities are nugatory, since they occur on the unimportant first and third words, i.e. *feng, jiang, cao, she, qian.*

Within the category of the New Verse Style, the *jue-ju* or regulated quatrain, was of almost equal importance. Here once again, strict rules of tonal sequence, parallelism and antithesis were demanded. Since most great poets break the rules, I have first of all chosen, as an example of this genre and, simply to clarify the metrical pattern, a composition of my own. It was originally composed to illustrate classical prosody for my second-year students, and laments the pollution of the noble city of Edinburgh by traffic fumes. Chinese poets would perhaps have approved the hortative motivation, but would hardly slap the table in admiration of its dubious artistry.

   L   L   L   O   O
Tuo shan heng gu bao
Hump mount straddles ancient burgh

   O   O   O   L   L
Du qi man xin cheng
Poison vapours fill New Town

   O   O   L   L   O
Si chu ting che xiang
Four places hear vehicle sounds

   L   L   O   O   L
Zhou za jian wu sheng
All around see fog rise.

Bad verse such as this baffles translation, as the following McGonagallesque attempt demonstrates:

> King Arthur's mount rides still above the burgh,
> But noxious vapours poison our New Town;
> I'm deafened by the traffic roaring on,
> And blinded by the fog that settles down.

The grammatical analysis of the prosody is as follows:

> Hump mount straddles ancient burgh
> *Noun noun verb adjective noun*
> Poison vapours fill New Town
> *Noun noun verb adjective noun*
> Four-places hear vehicle sounds
> *Adverb-phrase verb noun verb*
> All-around see fog rise
> *Adverb-phrase verb noun verb*

There is of course antithesis and parallelism in the first couplet and the second, and lines two and three are tonally complementary to each other on the second and fourth words. Rhyme too is predictably orthodox, being at the end of the first and second couplets.

For a more worthwhile but less orthodox example, let us turn to a seven-word regulated quatrain from this collection, i.e. 'A Warning to Censors' by Zhang Jie (see p. 90):

O O L   L O O L
Zhu bo yan xiao di ye xu   (R)
Bamboo silk smoke dissipate Emperor enterprise empty
  L L L*   L* O L L
Guan he kong xiao zu long ju   (R)
Pass river vain block grandfather dragon residence
  L L O   O L   L   O
Kang hui wei leng shan dong luan
Pit ash not-yet cold Shan Dong confusion
L* O   L   L O O L
Liu Xiang yuan lai bu du shu   (R)
Liu and Xiang originally not read books.

The syllables with asterisks represent divergences from the norm, of which only *xiao* in line two would be considered a radical break with conventional prosody, since the other two irregularities occur in the first and third words of a line. The rhyme-scheme follows the standard pattern of seven-word regulated quatrains, i.e. *a, a, b, a*. Here again, however, *shu* is not a 'good' rhyme for *xu* and *ju*, whose vowels are more or less equivalent to French *u* or German *ü*. There is little attempt at grammatical parallelism in the first couplet, but *di ye* (Emperor enterprise) and *zu long* (grandfather dragon) are both grammatically parallel and antithetical in meaning. The first hints at good government, i.e. an imperial design; and this is contrasted with abuse of power, conveyed by the traditional pejorative term for the First Emperor of the Qin Dynasty, 'Grandfather Dragon'. Similarly, in the last couplet *Pit, ash* (Noun/noun) contrasts with and complements *Liu, Xiang* (Proper noun/Proper noun), where an association is achieved by way of a reference to the historical events surrounding the short-lived Qin Dynasty: the entombment of scholars, the burning of books and the subsequent civil war, following the collapse of the dynasty, fought between the usurpers Liu Bang and Xiang Yu.

Under the category of verse with an irregular number of words to a line come a host of strange bed-fellows, ranging from the other great early corpus of poetry, the *Songs of the South* of the late Zhou Dynasty (not included in this anthology), the prose-poem or *fu*, the *ci* and its offshoot the *San Qu*, and most later folk-song genres—drum ballads (*gu-ci*), lute ballads (*tan-ci*), and the generic term 'rustic song' or *Shan Ge*. Practically the one denominator common to all these types of verse, is that such poems have lines of varying length.[2] The very fact that they are often bundled together in unhappy union reflects a traditional Chinese tendency towards baffling syncretism.

Of course there is a stronger case to be made for linking *ci* and *San Qu*. Historically we can trace the origins of *San Qu*

---

[2] Even this is not always the case, e.g. the *ci* tune *Sheng cha zi* is made up of eight lines of five words each.

to the later forms of ci. But even these last two categories are tremendously rich in divergency of prosodic forms themselves. Wang Li lists over two hundred metrical patterns alone for the ci lyrics.[3] Obviously with such a number of variations for ci I can only make a random selection[4] here, and list one of several tune patterns included in this anthology. When a Chinese poet composed a ci, unless he also composed a totally original tune of his own he would normally write his poem to an existing tune or air faithfully fitting his words to the metre and tone pattern of the original. This process was called 'tian ci', or filling in the lyrics. Many ci are untitled, but simply listed under the title of the melody to which the poet had composed his words. Thus when Xin Qi-ji wrote the ci which we have entitled 'Left-Overs', he chose to substitute new words for the old song 'West River Moon'. Once having made his choice he was obliged to conform to the metrical pattern of the original, but had he felt constrained by such a verse schema he might well have chosen any of numerous other ci patterns or even composed a new form of his own. Thus the ci, in spite of its metrical intricacies, in the last analysis represents a freer form of poetic composition than say the New Style cadenced and regulated verse.

Let us look at the metrical breakdown of Xin Qi-ji's poem, prefaced by the translation, which does not attempt to reproduce the intricate pattern of the original:

When drunk just stick to happiness
I ask you, who's for sorrow?
Recently I've had a feeling
　—those good old books
They're not so good, you know.

On the drink again last night
By a pine tree down I tumbled
'I'm really drunk, you know,'
　I tell old pine

[3] For more detailed discussion of ci see A Collection of Chinese Lyrics by A. Ayling and D. Mackintosh, Routledge and Kegan Paul, London, 1965.
[4] Wang Li, Han-yu Shi-lü-xue, Peking, 1962.

Who moves to pick me up
   or so it seemed.
Out came my hands
   'Clear off,' I said.

1. Zui-li qie tan huan-xiao
      Yao chou na-de gong fu.   (R)
      Jin lai shi jue gu-ren shu   (R)
      Xin zhu quan wu shi chu.   (R)

2. Zuo ye song bian zui dao
      Wen song 'wo zui he-ru'   (R)
      Zhi yi song dong yao lai fu   (R)
      Yi shou tui song yue 'qu'   (R)

It will be seen that there are exactly fifty words in this poem,
aportioned between two identically patterned verses, each of
four lines, with six words in the first second and fourth lines
and seven in the third. The rhyme scheme is as follows: *a, b,
b, b; a* or *c, b, b, b*. Note too that though lines 2, 3 and 4 rhyme,
the rhyme of the last word of the last line in each verse is an
oblique tone form unlike the other two. In *shi* verse of the New
Verse genre, rhymes were invariably the same tone through-
out, and even then very few *shi* of the genuine cadenced or
regulated variety can be found with oblique rhymes.

Superficially, at least, the *San Qu* verse, which flourished
from the thirteenth century onwards, seems to differ not so
very radically from the *ci*, for like its antecedent it was a
verse composed to a particular melody, and where rhyme and
tone pattern followed that of the original lyrics. Yet the
tunes, rhyme and tone patterns to which *San Qu* verses were
composed were totally different from those of the *ci*. Often
the melodies to which the *qu* were sung had their origins in
the music of Central Asia, and were imported by the Tartars

165

and Mongols during their conquest of China. Since *qu* developed in the North, with its new capital at Da Du (or Peking), they were composed in the northern dialect, which later became the linguafranca throughout the Empire, and remains the national language of China to this day. The tonal structure of Northern Chinese differed from the more archaic language on which *shi* and *ci* had been based. In *shi* and *ci* the primary distinction had been between oblique and level tones, whereas *qu* verse had a totally new metrical system based on the four tones of Northern Chinese. Altogether the *qu* was a more vigorous colloquial form than the *ci*, with a natural pace and rhythm derived from the vernacular in which it was often written.[5]

One of the many popular *San Qu* forms was the tune known as 'Hong Xiu Xie' (Red Embroidered Shoes), also referred to as 'Zhu Lü Qu' (The Vermilion Slipper Air). It is not surprising that such a tune with its (fetishistic) overtones, to the Chinese of the fourteenth century at least, was frequently chosen as the pattern tune for verses whose subjects were of an erotic or bawdy nature. In this anthology the poem on p. 125 entitled 'Unruly Sun' by Guan Yun-shi was written to this air.[6]

The writer of *San Qu* verse unlike those of *ci* was free to insert extraneous words into his lines. Such words are called *Chen-zi* (padded words), and they are frequently difficult to detect unless one is already familiar with the tune pattern, for though not essential to the burden of the poem, they rarely if ever entirely distort the basic meaning of a particular line.

In the following transliteration and word-for-word translation of Guan Yun-shi's poem, I have underlined all the 'padded words'; the actual syllable-count and rhyme-scheme is *6a, 6a, 7a, 5b, 5a, 5a.*

[5] For more detailed information on the prosody of *San Qu*, see the article by Dr. Wayne Schlepp in *Wen Lin, Studies in the Chinese Humanities*, Wisconsin University Press, Madison, Wis., 1968, entitled 'Metrics in Yüan San-ch'ü'.

[6] For an actual example of the reconstructed musical score of this tune see Richard Yang, David Liang and Myrtle Yang, 'Poetic Songs of the Yüan', *Chinese Culture*, vol. 11, no. 1, Taiwan, 1970.

Ai zhe kao zhe yun chuang tong zuo,
Nest(ling), lean(ing) cloud window together sit
Kan zhe xiao zhe yue zhen shuang ge.
Look(ing) laugh(ing) moon pillow together sing
Ting zhe shu zhe pa zhe chou zhe zao si geng guo.
Listen(ing) count(ing) fear(ing) sorrow(ing)
   (early) four watch pass
Si geng guo qing wei zu.
(Four) watch pass love not yet enough
Qing wei zu ye ru suo
(Love) not yet enough night like (a) shuttle
Tian ne, geng run yi geng fang shen mo?
(Heaven oh make more leap) one watch hurt what thing?

By comparing this crude literal version with the translation which follows, one can see how in this particular case the padded words can be easily embodied in the translation without its sounding too contrived:

Nestling, leaning by the cloud window both we sit
Looking, smiling on the moon pillow in tune we sing
Listening, counting, fearing, sorrowing, early comes the
   dawn drum
The fourth stroke's past, our passion's not yet quenched
Our passion's not yet quenched, night like a shuttle
O sky, just one more leap-hour, where's the harm?

Other *San Qu* verses with their plethora of rhythmic 'padded words' are less obliging to a translator. Perhaps the nearest equivalent of this poetic phenomenon a Westerner is likely to be familiar with is the improvised phases often interpolated between lines by a blues singer.

Bibliography to Appendix

Baxter, Glen William, 'Metrical Origins of the Tz'u', from *Studies in Chinese Literature* by John L. Bishop, Harvard University Press, Cambridge, Mass., 1965.

Chen Shih-chuan, 'The Rise of the Tz'u, Reconsidered', *Journal of the American Oriental Society*, vol. 90, no. 2, April-June, 1970.

Downer, G. B. and Graham, A. C., 'Tone Patterns in Chinese Poetry', *Bulletin of the School of Oriental and African Studies*, vol. 26, no. 1, 1963.

Hoffman, A., 'Kurze Einführung in die Technik der San-chü', *Chung Te Hsüeh-chih*, vol. 5, nos. 1–2, Peking, 1943.

Huang Xu-wu, *Shi-ci-qü cong-tan*, Singapore, 1969.

Johnson, Dale R., 'The Prosody of Yüan Drama', *T'oung Pao* (Archives), vol. 56, Leiden, 1970.

Li Shen, *Gu-dian Shi-ge chang-shi*, Hong Kong, 1968.

Liu Mau-tsai, 'Das Bild in der Dichtung der T'ang Ziet', *Oriens Extremis*, vol. 16, no. 2, December 1969.

Qu Tui-yuan and Zhon Zi-yi, *Xue-shi qian-shuo*, Hong Kong, 1967.

Schlepp, Wayne, 'Metrics in Yüän San-ch'ü', in *Wen-Lin, Studies in the Chinese Humanities*, edited by Tse-tsung Chow, University of Wisconsin Press, Madison, Wis. 1968.

Wang Li, *Han-yu shi-lü-xue*, Shanghai, 1963.

Whitaker, K. P., 'Source Notes on the Tsyr', *Bulletin of the School of Oriental and African Studies*, vol. 14, pt. I, 1952.

Wu Xuan-tau, *Gu-dian shi-ge ru-men*, Hong Kong, 1963.

Yang, Richard, Liang, David and Yang, Myrtle, 'Poetic Songs of the Yüan', *Chinese Culture* (A Quarterly Review), vol. 11, no. 1, 1970. (This article presents a tentative reconstruction of some of the original musical scores and tunes of the *San Qu*, including the tune 'Red Embroidered Shoes'.)